Y0-BLT-629

# BY
# DIVINE
# DESIGN

Other Books by BettyClare Moffatt

*An Authentic Woman:
Soulwork for the Wisdom Years*

*The Caregiver's Companion:
Words to Comfort and Inspire*

*Journey toward Forgiveness:
Finding Your Way Home*

*A Soulworker's Companion:
A Year of Spiritual Discovery*

*Opening to Miracles:
True Stories of Blessings and Renewal*

*Soulwork: Clearing the Mind, Opening the Heart,
Replenishing the Spirit*

*Gifts for the Living: Conversations with
Caregivers on Death and Dying*

*AIDS: A Self-Care Manual
(Editor and Contributor)*

*When Someone You Love Has AIDS:
A Book of Hope for Family and Friends*

*Looking Good: A Woman's Guide
to Personal Unfoldment*

# BY DIVINE DESIGN

*Awaken Your Spiritual Power*

BettyClare Moffatt

KENSINGTON BOOKS
http://www.kensingtonbooks.com

KENSINGTON BOOKS are published by

Kensington Publishing Corp.
850 Third Avenue
New York, NY 10022

Copyright © 2000 by BettyClare Moffatt

All rights reserved. No part of this book may be reproduced in any form or by any means without the prior written consent of the Publisher, excepting brief quotes used in reviews.

Kensington and the K logo Reg. U.S. Pat. & TM Off.

Library of Congress Card Catalogue Number: 99-066834
ISBN 1-57566-539-5

First Printing: April, 2000
10  9  8  7  6  5  4  3  2  1

Printed in the United States of America

*To the memory of Charles Fillmore,*

*1854–1948,*

*founder of Unity,
whose words inspire me*

Grateful acknowledgment is expressed to Unity School of Christianity for permission to use the original seed material contained in this book. This material originally appeared in the early 1900s as supplementary exercises to Charles Fillmore's book *The Twelve Powers of Man* (1930). It was presented then as "the greatest key to logical and rational expression of spiritual man that has ever been given to the public." Retitled *Christ Enthroned in Man,* the work was reprinted serially in *Unity Magazine* in 1974 and then reprinted for study groups at Unity. Cora Fillmore revised the original material to present it more clearly in its booklet form. I have used the original meditations for this present book, as well as quotations from the original book, *The Twelve Powers of Man*, in order to help spiritual seekers access, develop, and strengthen their inner powers through this uniquely Western system of spiritual development.

# Contents

*Preface xiii*

*How to Use This Book xix*

*Introduction*
*The Energy Centers: The Twelve Spiritual Powers and How to Use Them 1*

*Chapter One*
*The Spiritual Power of Faith*
   *Location: Center of Brain.*
   *Disciple: Peter 19*

*Chapter Two*
*The Spiritual Power of Strength*
   *Location: Loins. Disciple: Andrew 30*

*Chapter Three*
*The Spiritual Power of Discrimination or Judgment*
   *Location: Pit of Stomach. Disciple: James, Son of Zebedee 39*

*Chapter Four*
*The Spiritual Power of Love*
   *Location: Back of Heart. Disciple: John 48*

x / Contents

## Chapter Five
The Spiritual Power of Power
  Location: Root of Tongue.
  Disciple: Philip  57

## Chapter Six
The Spiritual Power of Imagination
  Location: Between the Eyes. Disciple:
  Bartholomew  64

## Chapter Seven
The Spiritual Power of Understanding
  Location: Front Brain. Disciple: Thomas  75

## Chapter Eight
The Spiritual Power of Will
  Location: Center Front Brain.
  Disciple: Matthew  84

## Chapter Nine
The Spiritual Power of Order
  Location: Navel. Disciple: James,
  Son of Alphaeus  92

## Chapter Ten
The Spiritual Power of Zeal
  Location: Back of the Head, Medulla.
  Disciple: Simon the Canaanite  99

## Chapter Eleven
The Spiritual Power of Renunciation or
  Elimination
  Location: Abdominal Region.
  Disciple: Thaddaeus   105

## Chapter Twelve
The Spiritual Power of Generative Life
  Location: Generative Function.
  Disciple: Judas   115

## Conclusion
The Twelve Spiritual Powers United   126

Suggestions for Further Study   134

# Preface

*"Spiritual discernment always precedes demonstration."*

*By Divine Design* is a series of spiritual exercises, originally developed as a workbook to accompany the writings of Charles Fillmore, a nineteenth-century metaphysical minister and the founder of Unity. I have worked with this material for almost thirty years.

In the early 1970s, I began to study and utilize Unity principles in order to heal and change my life. Later, I wrote for *Unity Magazine* and taught classes at my local New Thought church, Truth Guidelines. I also wrote for other New Thought magazines (*Science of Mind* and *New Thought Quarterly*). Later still, as a publisher, I brought New Thought ideas to the public via *The Law of Mind in Action,* an early text of Fenwicke Lindsey Holmes (cofounder with his brother, Ernest Holmes, of the Religious Science movement and *Science of Mind* magazine) which I edited with Dr. Margie Ann Nicola, my minister at Unity-By-The-Sea, in Santa Monica, California. I also edited and published *Master Meditations: A Spiritual Daybook,* by Dr. Donald Curtis, a well-known Unity minister and spiritual writer. Later still, I used my thirty-year spiritual journey to write (among many other books) *Soulwork: Clearing the Mind, Opening the Heart, Replenishing the Spirit; Opening to Miracles: True Stories of Blessings and Renewal; Journey toward Forgiveness: Finding Your Way Home; A Soulworker's Companion: A Year of Spiritual Discovery;* and *An Authentic Woman: Soulwork for the Wisdom Years.* Excerpts from these books appeared in *Unity Magazine,* as well as other spiritual magazines. Each book taught me universal life lessons. Each book opened the way for the next. We write what we most need to understand.

The wheel has come full circle. Here I am, almost thirty years older than when I first discovered and began to apply this uniquely Western spiritual system of soul development. Along the way, I have written books that appeared, on the surface, to be the farthest thing from the original principles that Unity teaches. I wrote about AIDS, death and dying, grief recovery, and caregiving. I wrote about the tragedies and losses of human life, and the triumphs and opportunities inherent in those dark times of our lives. I wrote about finding strength and faith within the deepest challenges of our lives. These books are epiphanies for me. They clarify the ways in which a strong foundation of spiritual development steadies and strengthens each of us throughout the turbulence of a changing and chaotic world.

I am still learning my spiritual lessons. Three years ago, after an initiatory, transformative dream, I came upon my old copy of *Christ Enthroned in Man,* complete with my markings and scribbles on every page, dog-

Preface / xv

eared corners, and my occasional exclamation "Yes!" in the margin. I searched for the original text from which the *Christ Enthroned in Man* material originated, and found again a book I had studied years ago on my spiritual quest. It was *The Twelve Powers of Man*, a classic text on spiritual self-development by Charles Fillmore, the founder of Unity. I decided then to renew my own spiritual foundation by studying these messages and incorporating them into my daily life. This has brought me deep satisfaction and rich rewards.

I have been given written permission by Unity School of Christianity to translate this original seed material, originally called *The Twelve Powers of Man*, and its workbook exercises, originally called *Christ Enthroned in Man*, into a book of contemporary yet universal spiritual meditations that encompass a unique system of Western spiritual development. These meditations are based on twelve inner centers of spiritual power within the body (similar, in some cases, to the basic seven chakras of Eastern meditation). Taking the original material several steps further, I rewote the original meditations and added my own commentaries, using the elements of character development, right motivation, and service as guidelines to help the reader develop each spiritual center through prayer and meditation. The result is an entirely new book, presenting a system of practical spirituality that can be used daily by spiritual seekers from many different traditions.

The first paragraph of the original introduction to the book reads:

xvi / Preface

> "We must not go into this book blindly, for it is a potential dynamo for each one who tries to practice the spiritual exercises contained in it. Man's energy centers are his life, and intelligent treatment of these is essential not only to spirituality, but, more important, to his survival."

A woman's energy centers are her life, too. I remember vividly crossing out every reference to Man and Mankind in the original text when I first studied it, and putting She, Her, Woman, or my name instead. I wanted to incorporate the truths of this book into my life and spiritual work as a woman, and deplored the old-fashioned standard language of the generic Man and Mankind. I longed for a system of spiritual development that I could relate to as a woman. I wanted spiritual womankind, instead of mankind. I want it still. Yet I am more tolerant now. Spiritual development comes in all shapes, sizes, colors, genders. The Twelve Powers of Man are the Twelve Powers of Woman as well.

But woman finds her own divine design. The original language of the classic text, as well as my interpretations, explanations, expansions, and meditations are, I devoutly hope, sensitive to the language of spiritual womankind, as well as traditional mankind. Whenever possible, I have substituted feminine pronouns in place of the generic exhortations to Man and Mankind, since this is a book whose intention is based on connecting to the emerging spiritual woman. It took me some time to find my way delicately and prayerfully through the original material,

Preface / xvii

while shaping, in my own voice, a new form that honors the original text even as it brings the spiritual practices contained within it into the twenty-first century. The quotations that anchor each of the chapters in this book come from *The Twelve Powers of Man*, while the meditations are rewritten from the *Christ Enthroned in Man* material.

Often it seemed I was grafting new limbs onto the sturdy trunk of an ancient wisdom tree. It was Charles Fillmore himself who said, in many of his spiritual books, that his current interpretation was subject to change as he grew in understanding. Often, when I did not know how to proceed in interpreting the traditional material for new readers, I would practice the meditations within the original text. I would use the meditations as a focus for other work that I was doing, other books I was writing, other responsibilities I was struggling with. I had first used these meditations almost thirty years earlier. Certainly I had to regrow into the material with my own daily private spiritual practice. I practiced these spiritual exercises sitting, standing, walking. I repeated them on early morning walks, using the rhythm of my feet to ground me in spiritual understanding. (Metaphysically, the feet planted firmly on the ground symbolize understanding.) I am still learning, still growing, still understanding the Twelve Powers and the symbolism of Christ Enthroned within. It seemed to me then, and it seems to me now, that the words offer a design for living. A divine design.

Some people who read this book may wish for more

Christian symbolism, and may take issue with Unity's emphasis on God within each one of us. Other people may find that their belief systems conflict with the ancient ideas of God, Jesus Christ, and the Holy Spirit, preferring instead to use the words *Higher Power, Higher Consciousness, Oneness, Great Creator,* or as is often the custom in Unity literature, *Dear Mother–Father–God.* Others may find an old-fashioned quality in the original text, remembering that it was written almost 100 years ago, and came out of the Emersonian roots of the great American Transcendentalist movement, as well as the ideas of early metaphysical teachers, such as those that the Fillmores knew personally and studied with while developing their own spiritual system of Christian mysticism that forms the basis of the Unity prayer movement. Words have great currrency and power in spiritual literature, and you may choose to substitute your own words while practicing the meditations. There are many roads to spiritual awareness. This is one.

What shines forth from the original text is much more than "Christ Enthroned in Man." It is "God Enthroned in All." God woven within woman and man, God incorporated within each of us, person, place, or thing. It is the "invisible beyond the visible world" that each of us can develop and embrace.

By divine design we open to the words within this book. By divine design we are changed and quickened and healed. By divine design we become the spiritual Self we have always longed to become. By divine design we come home to the best within ourselves. By divine design, we come home to God.

# How to Use This Book

*"To desire to be instructed by God is the first step in exalting the inner life force. The sincere desire of the heart is always fulfilled by the divine law."*

*By Divine Design* can be used as a solitary spiritual practice or as part of a prayer group, support group, or workshop. Continuing individual study is recommended on a daily basis, even when working weekly with a group. Daily spiritual practice is a discipline that can yield rich rewards.

You can practice the spiritual exercises sitting upright in a straight-backed chair, feet planted firmly on the ground, head erect, legs uncrossed, hands resting on the knees, with open palms upturned to receive. Your eyes may initially be open to read the text. When an exercise is memorized or read aloud in a group setting, the eyes are closed in prayer. Or if you are familar with Yoga practices or any type of Eastern meditation, you can sit cross-legged on the floor, back upright, with the thumb and the second finger of the hand making a circle, as your arms rest on your crossed knees. These exercises can be practiced kneeling, with palms together, as in traditional Christian prayer. They can also be practiced standing erect, feet planted firmly on the floor, hands held loosely at the sides of the body, or rising with the sound of the declarations spoken aloud. You can even practice a meditation-in-motion form, in which you repeat the exercises silently as you walk. You can lie down to practice the exercises, but this is recommended only if you are ill or very tired. Even if you practice the exercises at night just before you go to bed, it is best to stay awake and alert during your spiritual practice, and to surround yourself with light and healing as you go to sleep, repeating your favorite prayer as desired.

I strongly suggest a daily spiritual discipline of arising before dawn, when the world is quiet and most people are asleep, and spending an initial fifteen minutes a day practicing these spiritual exercises. The time may extend up to an hour, combined with other spiritual reflections and movement practices as you advance in spiritual concentration. Begin by practicing at least five days a week. When you skip days, you will notice the difference in your body, mind, emotions, and spirit. Your life will be transformed by the continual daily practice of meditation and prayer. You can, if you wish, incorporate these exercises into an existing meditation routine. They work well with breathing exercises, Yoga, Chi Gong, T'ai Chi, or any other movement practice, such as walking.

Some people have found it beneficial to break their practice into two daily times of reflection—one in the early morning, the other in the late afternoon or before bedtime. Sometimes only a few minutes of spiritual concentration are required for a peaceful, creative day. When under great stress, you can practice any or all of the exercises as ongoing prayer. There is no wrong way to open to Spirit.

Why a disciplined and ongoing system of spiritual exercises? You are building a core self of spiritual strength that will serve you well through all the difficulties and all the joys of a well-lived, creative life. You are also building a relationship with your Creator, by whatever name you call God, from Jesus Christ, to Divine Teacher, to Holy Spirit, to Oneness.

For now, just begin. One exercise at a time, one breath at a time, one insight at a time, one change at a time, one prayer at a time. You will be gently led.

*Introduction*

# The Energy Centers: The Twelve Spiritual Powers and How to Use Them

*"Through mental energy, or the dynamic power of the mind, [you] can release the life of the electrons secreted in the atoms that compose the cells of [your] body."*

Everything is energy. And since we are energy beings, living in a sea of energy, the task before us is to learn various methods of awakening, controlling, and utilizing the divine energy within us and all around us. This involves the physiological as well as the psychological and the spiritual.

There are centers within each of us that can be awakened. Indeed, we are using these energy centers all the time, whether we realize it or not.

These centers of power have been known for thousands of years, but not until recently have they come into general awareness. Before, they were esoteric and hidden. Now, even scientists confirm the existence of various centers of energy in and around the physical body. There is continuing debate over how many centers there are and where such centers are located, although the endocrine glands have long been identified as the physical counterparts of some of the ancient energy centers. Classical Yoga literature identifies seven such centers, called chakras (wheels of power, wheels of light, wheels of energy).

However, few people know of the existence of a form of Western spiritual development that identifies and utilizes twelve spiritual centers within the body. These spiritual centers conform, in many cases, to the exact locations of the Eastern chakras, with some additions. These twelve spiritual centers correspond to twelve soul qualities that must be developed in an awakened life. The twelve soul qualities are called the twelve disciples. According to Charles Fillmore, the founder of Unity, these twelve gateways to spiritual consciousness can be awakened and energized through disciplined prayer. The twelve powers, in ascending order through the body, are: life, elimination (renunciation), order, strength, wisdom, love, power, zeal, faith, imagination, understanding, and will, culminating in the encirclement of the top of the head in Christ Consciousness (very similar to the seventh chakra at the top of the head, which is a manifestation of divine consciousness in the Eastern chakra system of development).

Here are the twelve powers, and the names of the corresponding twelve disciples, as interpreted in *The Twelve Powers of Man:*

Introduction: The Energy Centers / 3

Faith—Peter—center of brain.
Strength—Andrew—loins.
Discrimination or Judgment—James, son of Zebedee—pit of stomach.
Love—John—back of heart.
Power—Philip—root of tongue.
Imagination—Bartholomew—between the eyes.
Understanding—Thomas—front brain.
Will—Matthew—center front brain.
Order—James, son of Alphaeus—navel.
Zeal—Simon the Canaanite—back of head, medulla.
Renunciation or Elimination—Thaddaeus—abdominal region.
Generative Life—Judas—generative function.

You do not have to profess a certain faith in order to benefit from these spiritual exercises. Spiritual consciousness knows no dogma or denomination. The above twelve gateways, with their corresponding locations, qualities, and disciples, are merely words on a map. It is what you do with the energies, as you gradually access the light contained within each center, that will determine your awakening.

In addition, Chinese literature speaks of meridians (like those used in acupuncture) with literally hundreds of energy points diagrammed throughout the body. The various martial arts disciplines also identify centers of energy within the body—such as the ki, or chi, which corresponds and resides just under the navel center. In my

4 / BY DIVINE DESIGN

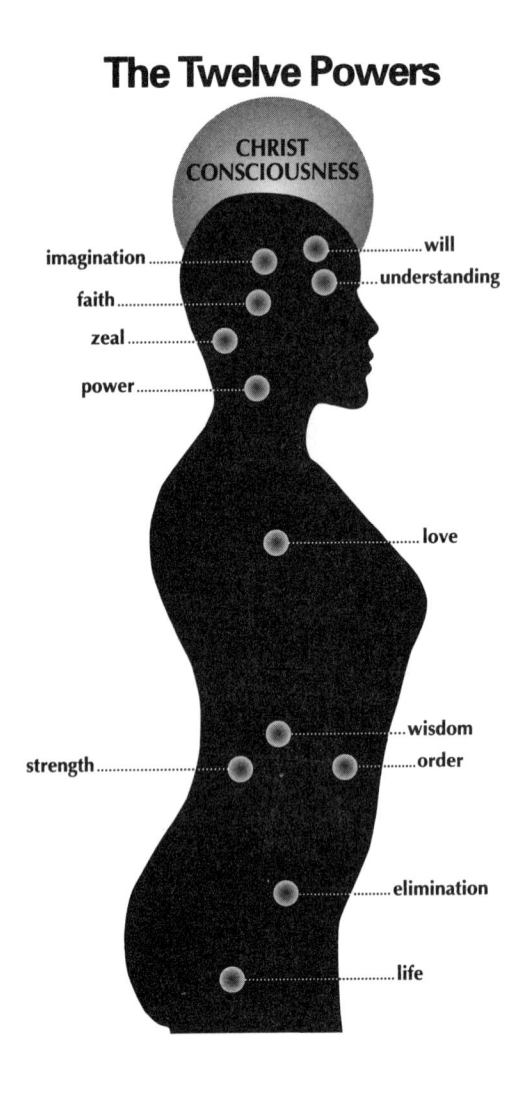

# The Twelve Powers

CHRIST CONSCIOUSNESS

- imagination
- will
- understanding
- faith
- zeal
- power
- love
- wisdom
- strength
- order
- elimination
- life

ongoing workshops and study of Kundalini Yoga, I learned of many other chakra centers besides the classic ones mentioned above. Current literature now suggests that there are myriad centers of energy within the body that can be accessed, energized, and brought to greater awareness.

The existence of these energy centers is too persuasive to ignore. They are more than a physical manifestation, although they may express themselves through various glands and channels within the bodily system. They are mystical centers, gateways to awareness, gateways to the infinite. Through serious study and faithful meditation, these energy centers can produce healing at the soul level within a person. While traditional spiritual literature cautions that these energy centers should be awakened only under the guidance of a teacher, I have found that anyone who meditates sincerely for any sustained period of time, with a prayerful intent for good, eventually has access to these centers of power.

All the energy exercises lead to an inner awakening, an inner knowing that you will develop knowledge as you explore your own incredible, mysterious, unique, glorious potential. The more you read and practice the simple, safe spiritual exercises in this book, the more gently and thoroughly your own inner energy will flower.

## ✣ Do Not Rush. Do Not Force.

As long as you are clear about your purpose and as long as you prepare your system physically (one reason for the need for Yoga and other meditation-in-motion exercises), you will be gently led to your own unique path, your own best way of being and doing in the world. The more you know about the ways in which your total energy system works, the easier it will be for you to accept and to experience the intuitive, the creative, the joy behind the visible, outward universe. It is this invisible energy, this matrix of thought and feeling and spiritual perception, that determines your actions and reactions, the way you see yourself and others, the way you conduct your life or acquiesce in allowing someone else to run it for you. The power is in you. How you use your power and your energy determines your destiny and creates your own divine design.

## ✣ Spiritual Steps

> *"All those who are following Spirit are finding it necessary to move out of a three-dimensional consciousness into a four-dimensional consciousness. This is the process known as transformation."*

How do you move out of an ordinary three-dimensional consciousness into one that sees beyond the material, exterior world and into the heart of Spirit? In addition to the meditations throughout the book, we will look at every aspect of who we are, go through spiritual clearing steps, and learn how to reshape our lives into a divine design. We will begin with three steps that Fillmore considered crucial to transformation. These are:

- Character building
- Right and selfless motivation
- Service

Fillmore tells us:

"As for character, each of us, by observing the self in action from moment to moment, becomes aware of strengths and deficiencies in the areas of his or her energies—physical, emotional, and occasionally at a deeper level of soul response. With a daily spiritual practice, the soul awakens and begins to gain ascendency over its swirling currents of energy. As the soul begins to control the energies surrounding itself, it gains in spiritual strength and virtue. As the soul learns how to control the denser energies and 'bodies' surrounding itself, it builds character."

I had never considered that it was the soul's responsibility to help the spiritual seeker to develop a wise and loving character structure. Yet as I began to work daily with meditation and prayer, and ask daily for spiritual help, I began to see that it was not just my own human physical body, my emotional desires, and my own determined mental will that would help me to understand and to grow spiritually. It was my soul calling out to me.

Right motivation is also essential to any genuine awakening of one's energy centers. What is your primary motive in seeking the spiritual? What do you hope to gain from spiritual practice? Fame? Fortune? Love? Control? Power? There is nothing wrong with wanting the very best for yourself and your loved ones, but the external manifestations of good in your life cannot and must not be your primary motive for seeking spiritual understanding.

According to Fillmore:

> "Any quest for spiritual development and illumination can take place genuinely only when followed out of love for God, when you live wholly so that His will is done."

Finally, any spiritual aspiration must involve the idea of service. This is a somewhat quaint, old-fashioned notion, yet every time I give a speech or attend a workshop, someone comes up to me and asks, "How can I make a difference in the world? How can I help?" I believe that there is a deep yearning within each of us to serve. According to Fillmore:

> "Each of us is primarily the servant of everyone else, and it is only as we are able to drop our com-

petitiveness to see ourselves more accurately as we really are, beyond wish or ideal, that we can begin to act selflessly out of service, beyond ambition. Such a life demands honesty and sincerity, devotion and struggle. Such a life is a new beginning. It is a door opening into a larger room."

When a dear friend of mine read the words above, he almost exploded in frustration. "What an old-fashioned, unrealistic way of looking at the world!" he cried. "Tell me how to make my life work in this cynical, complicated, speeded-up world, and then I'll pay attention." But after practicing the spiritual exercises, as delineated by Fillmore and adapted by me, he came to me and said, "I believe that I'm a good person, but I never thought much before about character, right motivation, and service. By practicing these exercises, I feel more peaceful, more centered, gentler with myself and others. Maybe there's something here for me to learn after all."

Yes, there is.

There is a saying in spiritual work that as you do the work of the soul with full intention, "Results follow after." First the soulwork, then and only then the outcome. You cannot worry about how things will work out, you cannot force external results according to your own ideas of how things should be. This is a lesson that we are all still learning.

You can change your life. You can heal your life. You can have great good in your life. But you start with the inner, not the outer. You start within, not without. When you change your consciousness, you change your world. And always, always, always, you start with the work of the soul.

Let go of all preconceptions of yourself. Let go of all ideas of what is wrong with the world and what is right with you. Let go of judgments and limitations. Then and only then will you begin to catch a glimpse, even for a moment, of another dimension, another way of looking at the world.

Then and only then can you begin to "dwell continuously in the finer spiritual dimension, where you see more clearly through the eyes of Spirit, hear with the ears of Spirit, and feel with the heart of Spirit." What a heroic task for anyone, man or woman, to undertake.

This is indeed the work of the soul. Results follow after.

## ✤ A Meditation on the God Consciousness or Christ Consciousness

> "Physical science says that if the electronic energy stored in a single drop of water were suddenly released, its power would demolish a six-story building. Who can estimate the power stored in the millions of cells that compose the human body?"

After realizing that you are first and foremost a spiritual being in both soul and body, the first step is never to

# Introduction: The Energy Centers / 11

lose contact with this feeling. Your spiritual center, the abode of the original seed of the Christ Consciousness within you, is located in the crown of the head.

Sit down, spine erect, feet planted firmly on the floor, hands resting upon your knees, palms opened to receive. Then center your attention in the crown of the head, the home of the Christ Consciousness within you.

---

## Affirm:

"The Christ Consciousness is awakening in me."

*As you realize this statement, remember that "the Christ" is the perfect-Son idea, God-Mind's perfect call to you, containing all wisdom and power. Do not concentrate too intensely at this point for more than a moment or two, at least not in the beginning. The power of the word in your exercise contacting the Christ Consciousness of God in you naturally causes an outpouring of the Holy Spirit, which is sometimes manifested in a soft golden light of pure intelligence. In some instances where a great spiritual realization is being released in consciousness, the light is white and dazzling as the sun. Allow this light to dissolve the darkness surrounding you, and let it expand within you as pure intelligence.*

*Now allow this Christ light to drop to the front*

*forehead, the seat of your daily, conscious mind. Affirm:*

"I am aware that the Christ Consciousness of God is awakening within me."

*At first you may not be aware of the soft golden light that is descending from the heights of your mind (the light is felt and not seen), but presently you will be able to feel this outpouring as an illumination, which gives you increased understanding. Then allow the Presence, the Christ light, to drop to the center of the head, the pineal gland. Then declare:*

"The Christ Consciousness of God through faith is awakening in me."

*In all the exercises that follow, remember to keep the conscious mind, which functions in the front forehead, awake to all that is going on and remain consciously aware through each continuous step in the spiritual unfoldment.*

*Also please note that the nose is a highly sensitive and intelligent organ. It symbolizes discernment, and it possesses a keen penetrating quality. Be sure the illumination of Spirit is penetrating into this organ as well, and that your discerning powers are quick, keen, and energetic.*

*From the high point of the crown of the head,*

*now allow the soft light of Spirit to flow down, down, down, penetrating and permeating every function and cell of the soul and body, down to the hands and feet. Consciously follow the light of Spirit down into the feet and even beneath the feet, with the heels especially receiving your attention. Dwell here for some time, fully aware of the flow of Spirit as pure illumination, awakening in you a greater degree of intelligence and light from the crown of the head to the soles of the feet.*

*With your attention centered in the feet, feel the windows of your soul open toward the heights of your mind. Be aware that you are saturated in holy light, the light of divine intelligence. You are wrapped in it as in a mantle, clothed from head to feet. This outpouring is known as the descending spiritual currrent.*

---

By now you may have discovered that there is also an ascending current of light energy coming up from the earth. In its original essence this ascending current was pure substance of Spirit. Now, however, it is mingled with the thoughts of the material world that each person must handle. Realize, then, that the descending current of Spirit does make its way entirely through the body temple, and it will contact the ascending current at various points to temper and harmonize all the undisciplined, denser thoughts of hate, fear, jealousy, lack, guilt, shame, resentment. With practice and patient attention to these two currents, you will feel them meeting within you more and more. You will receive greater insights into the truth of your being. You will better understand your problems and will learn how best to deal with them. You will find yourself raised to higher achievement and activity.

The descending spiritual current and the ascending earthly current, contacting each other at different points in soul and body consciousness, form centers of consciousness, located near different parts of the body. The most important of these centers is located in the region of the heart and stomach. Another one is located at the center of the base of the brain, the medulla. Minor points of contact are located at other centers with different powers or faculties.

The activity of divine intelligence in the descending spiritual current from above transforms the distorted error beliefs of the material world. These are contained in the earthly flow from beneath and are changed into constructive forces. This activity of divine intelligence gives the individual a richer and broader understanding of life in the manifest, earthly realm.

The ascending spiritual current, even while being transformed from above, continues its upward course, and is continuously contacting the never-ceasing descending spiritual flow. As you practice this spiritual exercise, you can feel yourself consciously ascending with this upward current to the point designated as the great distributing nerve center behind the heart and the stomach.

Introduction: The Energy Centers / 15

You will find that at this point you have a firmer grip on the power of the word and that the Christ Consciousness is setting up a throne of dominion here. In truth this is where the spiritual body begins its manifestation within the earthly body. Dwelling consciously here, call down from the heights of your mind all the powers: faith, strength, wisdom, love, will, understanding, imagination, zeal, power, order, renunciation, and life. Feel and affirm, silently or aloud, that these twelve powers (perfect ideas of substance in God-Mind) are entering your soul consciousness and organizing themselves as manifest substance at the very center of your being. Realize that their substance is being established throughout the whole soul and body. You are laying the foundation of the new Christ Consciousness or temple of God, with its twelve precious powers, which represent the intellectual perception of the spiritual body. At this point affirm and realize this invocation:

> "I am now in the presence of pure Being, immersed in the Holy Spirit of life, love, and wisdom. I acknowledge Thy presence and power, O blessed Spirit. In Thy divine wisdom I now erase my mortal limitations, and from Thy pure substance of love I bring my world into manifestation according to Thy perfect law."

After you have repeated this invocation, continue to realize that you are in the presence of the substance of pure Being and that you are immersed in the light of

Being. This light from on high saturates you from the crown of your head to the soles of your feet.

Then, in order that you may receive an even greater outpouring of the Holy Spirit, repeat very slowly the Lord's Prayer, as follows:

> *"Our Father Who art in heaven,*
> *Hallowed be Thy name.*
> *Thy kingdom come,*
> *Thy will be done, on earth as it is in heaven.*
> *Give us this day our daily bread;*
> *And forgive us our trespasses, as we forgive those who*
>   *trespass against us.*
> *And lead us not into temptation, but deliver us from*
>   *evil:*
> *For Thine is the kingdom, and the power, and the glory,*
>   *forever.*
> *Amen."*

These words connect the soul directly with the spiritual, celestial realm. With the Holy Spirit paramount in consciousness, both the vision and feeling natures are quickened. You now dwell consciously in your physical body, your soul body, and your spiritual body simultaneously. These three bodies are now being merged into one.

As you conclude the meditation, remain consciously alert to the meeting of spiritual currents going on within you. Stay alive to the working of Spirit, feel the light in

## Introduction: The Energy Centers / 17

your heart and head that is moving with wisdom and power. Be aware that you are gaining a firmer grip on the power of the word in the palms of your hands and in the soles of your feet between the ball of the foot and the heel. This practice tends to place you on a firm foundation and to give you a greater consciousness of the unfolding processes going on during the awakening of the permanent dwelling place of Spirit.

You are becoming a masterpiece. With the throne of the Christ Consciousness set up within the heart of your being, with the mantle of the Holy Spirit wrapped about you, and consciously cooperating with the one creative power of the universe, you become free to acquire a pure and perfect soul as well as a permanent and indestructible body temple.

*"God, Supreme Being, is the source out of which all creation evolves. God-Mind is an omnipresent spiritualized realm composed of creative ideas. Through continuous prayer and greater spiritual realization, you may make contact with these ideas, weave them into your soul consciousness, and create out of their substance the ideals of your heart."*

# Chapter One

# The Spiritual Power of Faith
# Location: Center of Brain
# Disciple: Peter

*"People who live wholly in the intellect deny that man can know anything about God, because they do not have quickened faith. The way to bring forth the God presence, to make oneself conscious of God, is to say: 'I have faith in God; I have faith in spirit; I have faith in things invisible.' Such affirmations of faith, such praise to the invisible God, the unknown God, will make God visible to the mind and will strengthen the faith faculty."*

AFFIRMATION: "The Holy Spirit is now here raising me to a consciousness of unfailing and eternal faith."

For many years, I attended Unity meditation classes on a regular basis and sought to develop my consciousness through regular spiritual practice from various traditions. One of the sayings that intrigued me was this one: "Fear knocked on the door. Faith answered. No one was there." I wondered how you develop faith—faith in yourself, faith in others, faith in a beneficent universe, faith in the outcomes of whatever challenges you are going through in your life. But most of all, I longed for an unwavering faith in God. Sometimes I felt this. Often I did not.

How can anyone tell anyone else exactly how to have faith in a supreme being? Faith, like the other soul qualities, must be accessed, awakened, developed by practice. It is the opposite of fear. I remember another saying that I used often when I first began working with spiritual qualities. It was the one about turning the word "fear," which is the opposite of faith, into an acronym. It went like this:

F—False
E—Evidence
A—Appearing
R—Real

As simple as this was, it brought me comfort. That is because when you re-language your habitual thoughts and fears, they become more manageable and can then be changed, first in thought, then in emotional intensity, then in spiritual trust. We will learn more about the power of re-languaging and re-imagining our thoughts, words, and actions as we go through the various spiritual exercises.

While some traditions of spiritual exercises start from

the ground up, move into the root center of a person, and rise from the lower to the higher, this system starts from the highest point in consciousness and works in spiraling currents all over the body. Fillmore felt strongly that by accessing the faith center and working from the crown consciousness downward, the light of Spirit would gradually uplift and transform the body temple and the mind and emotions as well. He saw faith as a beneficent protection to the spiritual seeker so that, when the twelve powers were gradually awakened, each person would be able to handle the various sense energies, instead of releasing a great flood of unresolved emotions and sensations before the body temple was ready to handle them. In fact, he counseled that after working with the first seven powers, a period of assimilation was needed before tackling the remaining five centers. In practice, however, he moved from center to center, up and down, front and back, working with the ascending and descending spiritual current. In some ways, his work corresponds to the teachings of Yoga, in which the aspirant learns to access and then direct the *ida* and the *pingala*, the ascending and descending currents that weave throughout the body temple on the wings of the breath.

Each exquisite cell in the body temple can be awakened, revealed, healed, and renewed. Each has its place in the overall pattern of your being. But by starting with the crown consciousness, we start with the light of the Holy Spirit descending into the body temple. Then one by one, we access the twelve powers, beginning with the faith center, which corresponds to the pineal gland, the traditional third eye center in Eastern spiritual systems.

At the center of the brain is the pineal gland. This gland is known to Truth students as the faith center, symbolized by the metaphysical disciple Peter, and faith is the "rock" upon which He founded His church. When the inner eye is illumined with spiritual faith, a ray of light—the pure white, pearly light of Spirit, steady and unwavering—is often seen in the silence. So unfaltering is this ray of the spiritual light of faith that it seems as unmovable as a star in the heavens. However, it is only a symbol, letting us know that the spiritual work has been done.

According to Fillmore:

> "Faith is: It is an attribute of God. Faith is purely spiritual, and it knows nothing less than complete assurance. Faith is dauntless; it does not know defeat. Faith is the quality of the mind that moves and molds ideas and brings them to concrete expression. Faith is the assurance or confidence of the mind that invisible substance is the source of all visible material things."

And yet so many people confuse the quality of faith with mere positive thinking. Nothing could be farther from the truth.

The difference between positive thinking and spiritual thinking is this: With positive thinking, you take baby

## The Spiritual Power of Faith / 23

steps in determining what you want out of life, what you want from others, what you want from yourself and your abilities. This is good and worthwhile. But then come various tests of faith. If you ask for spiritual understanding, if you ask to serve, if you ask to be more loving, if you ask to know God, you will indeed get your wish. You will move from baby steps to a progressive understanding of the work of the Spirit in your life. You will move from rote affirmations to an unshakable clearness, from wishful thinking to concrete action backed up by spiritual law.

The exercises in this book are not designed for positive thinking. They are designed by a master teacher to gently and powerfully awaken the whole Self—not the little self that longs for a bigger bank account, but the shining true Self that is your soul incarnate in your physical body. I remember someone once telling me that in order to move beyond positive thinking into spiritual thinking, I had to clear away "the whipped cream over the worms." For each step forward in spiritual understanding, there was a corresponding step in clearing away erroneous thinking, old patterns of resentment, hatred, rage, and cynicism, and especially, any patterns of unforgiveness of myself and others. The exercises in this book are not to be taken lightly, no matter how simple they may seem. When practiced prayerfully, with an open heart and a desire for increased faith and understanding, they will transform you.

Yet to learn to go from rote affirmations of peace, love, and plenty, in order to access and penetrate to the very heart of Spirit, is no easy task. So often people on a spiritual path confuse the saying with the soul's desire for wholeness. While letting go of old, worn-out, negative thought forms is an important phase in spiritual discernment, it is only one step on the spiritual path. To take the words of Fillmore and the affirmative prayers in this book and repeat them by rote will, of course, help you to understand and set up a routine of contemplative practice. But the very words "contemplative" and "practice," when put to use, tell us that we have far to go when using these twelve powers. In fact, we cannot use the twelve powers well until we have gone past the surface to the depths of their energy within us. We want to penetrate to the light within, to open to the light within, to access the light within. And each of these twelve powers is a light, an infusion and immersion of divine energy. We can and will begin to feel this energy instead of just saying the prayers. We will begin to bring meaning to these words, as they echo within us personally and prayerfully. We will begin to see how our prayer practice translates into our daily lives, as each inner action corresponds and reverberates into outer action.

You are working with the building blocks of light.

The first step is to have faith in the outcome of this practice.
The next step is the practice itself.
The third step is the gentle yet powerful manifestation of God working in your life.

## ❋ Questions and Responses

When working with the twelve powers of the soul, we need to appropriate them into our own consciousness, not only by practicing the meditations but by contacting the quality within us through questioning, listening, and then writing our answers.

- What does the word "faith" mean to you personally?
- Write three ways in which faith has shaped your life.
- Write three ways in which you intend to use the quality of faith in your life in the next month.

Before you practice the meditation on the faith center, please do the following:

Sit down quietly and look for the quality of faith within your body temple. Put your hand on the corresponding location where faith resides within you. Identify faith within you. What does it look like? How does it feel? If feelings of despair, grief, or inadequacy well up within you when you contemplate this quality (or its seeming lack), note the feeling and go forward. Ask aloud for more faith to be revealed to you. Ask for insights as to how you can develop and recognize more faith in your daily life. Ask for divine guidance. As you contemplate the quality of faith within you, notice if the place where faith resides changes in any way in order to respond to your intent. Does it feel warmer? More alive? Can you begin to feel what faith is? Ask that Faith be gently revealed to you in your life.

Then and only then practice the affirmative prayer spiritual exercise on faith. Let the words echo and penetrate your body temple. Continue to affirm your growing, living faith.

## ❦ Meditation

*Purpose*: To illuminate our consciousness until we realize that we have penetrated into the four-dimensional realm, through the material to the kingdom of the heavens.

For the beginning of this exercise, repeat the whole of the I AM exercise given in the Introduction. With the attention still at the great nerve center, take up the thought of infinite faith.

### Affirm:

"The faith of Almighty God is quickened within me."

After you have gained a better realization of Omnipresence as faith, follow the radiance of Spirit that leads to the faith center, the pineal gland, at the middle of the head. Then realize this same prayer:

"Through the awakening of Christ Consciousness the faith of Almighty God is quickened within me."

## The Spiritual Power of Faith / 27

Be perfectly relaxed and receptive to Spirit, as you gradually become conscious of the spiritual power descending from the spiritual center, the crown of the head, showering you with new faith.

The tiny ray of pure light that is often discernible in the silence at the faith center is simply the result of the radiation or vibration of the word of faith upon which you are concentrating. When the power of the word reaches a certain degree of intensity, the light of faith becomes visible. Do not try to perceive this ray; by so doing you hinder your own unfolding. Do the spiritual work quietly, remaining perfectly poised and relaxed. God will take care of the results. Now allow the Presence to drop slowly down to the love center, just behind the heart, and declare:

"Faith works through love."

Then allow the Presence, the light of Spirit, to drop down into the soles of the feet, and repeat this declaration:

"Understanding faith is now expressed through me."

At the conclusion of the exercise, allow the Presence (while you continue to cooperate) to organize itself just behind the heart and stomach. Again realize: Faith works through love. During this realization, consciously know that the windows of your soul are more widely opened toward the heavens of your mind, that the spiritual light as pure illumination is descending upon you, and that through faith you are steadily developing your spiritual body. End the exercise first with a realization of larger, more infinite love for all life; then finish with the Lord's Prayer, speaking the words very slowly.

Remember to keep the conscious mind, which operates through the front forehead, fully aware of all that is taking place. After you have finished, affirm that your conscious mind is awakening and perceiving clearly every step of the way. At the close of the exercise, for the sake of balance, direct your attention consciously to the feet and even beneath the feet; also throw the attention down into the palms of the hands, realizing that faith must always be accompanied with works, that nothing is yours unless you express it.

At the close of this meditation (also at the close of all the other exercises that follow), as you go forth into your daily life, know that your new realizations are freely finding expression in and through you, especially through the breast—the vital center of expression being at the point in the thorax, the lower part of the sternum, where the last of the true ribs are attached to the sternum. Also realize that your words are growing in power and intelligence and that you are strengthening a center of expression at that point where the upper lip is joined onto the base of the nose. By recognizing this, you will find that your voice will develop a richness and trueness that you, as well as your friends, will notice. Also know that a new light (illumination) is penetrating the seat of the conscious mind (front forehead) and that even your brow radiates the light of Spirit.

> "Spiritually faith acts as a force that can only be described in scientific terms by seers and sages. Faith is one of the fundamental laws governing the universe and is directly related to the underlying substance of the universe."

## Chapter Two

# The Spiritual Power of Strength
# Location: Loins
# Disciple: Andrew

*"The strength here discussed is not physical strength alone, but mental and spiritual strength. All strength originates in Spirit; and the thought and the word spiritually expressed bring the manifestation."*

AFFIRMATION: "The Holy Spirit is now here raising me to a consciousness of sustaining strength, and I rest in joy and peace."

How do you regain your strength when you think you have lost it? Sometimes it's an external event or series of events that debilitates you. Sometimes it's the slow erosion of years with dreams deferred and then denied. Sometimes it's an inner exhaustion that makes you feel empty and numb. And sometimes it's a combination of all of the above.

In late 1998, after my mother had been ill for seven years, after books projects had fallen through for me, threatening my livelihood, and after a flood under my house, the very foundation of my house collasped. The structural engineers and the insurance company rallied to major repairs of my house foundation. But I knew better. I knew that my strength had run out, my optimism was at an end, my creativity had gone into hiding, and my tears would not stop flowing. My foundation had given way. It was time for a change.

With the help of friends and family, I moved temporarily to the California desert to work, while my house was being repaired and readied for sale. My sister and brother-in-law supervised the nursing home care of my mother, who by this time, could neither move nor speak, and who no longer knew who I was. A dear cousin drove me to the desert, where my oldest son's family lived, and I prepared to work there for a couple of months. I found a tiny unfurnished apartment on the second floor of an old building surrounding a courtyard of palm trees, citrus trees, and flowers; and with a worktable, an office chair, my computer, and a daybed, I settled in.

Almost every day, when my work was done (and often when it wasn't), I would go to a small outdoor café on the main boulevard and sit there, notebook open, a glass of iced tea in front of me, and stare into space. I looked at the mountains. They were there on three sides of the valley floor, rising in tier after tier, changing colors as the day wore on. Wherever you go in the Coachella Valley, that enclave of sunshine and small towns and resorts, you are surrounded by mountains.

I needed those mountains. I hungered and thirsted

after their strength and grace and glory. I would say to myself every day, "I will lift up mine eyes unto the hills, whence cometh my help." I would say, "God is in the mountain and God is in me." I would amend this to say, "God's strength is in the mountains and God's strength is in me."

I had no monopoly on despair, exhaustion, or weakness. Most of the women and men that I know have experienced many challenging life lessons. At the time, though, I felt that I had had more than my fair share. I had run out of fingers to count my list of disappointments and responsibilities, accumulated over a twelve-year period of challenges. I felt weak and frightened. I needed inner strength and outer strength to sustain me. I found it in the mountains.

You may have other images that sustain you. Fillmore talks about soaring on wings of eagles, while other texts remind us of the root of the tree of life that sustains us. You may have other prayers and meditations as well. I had many wise words and heartfelt images to connect with.

It was at this time that I began again to reconnect with the spiritual principles that had sustained me throughout difficult times. I went back to core principles and to the inner core of myself. I began again to meditate, pray, and affirm, using the very words now found in this book.

By the end of winter, with the help of the sunshine, the mountains, and the core meditations that I brought to life inside me from the practice of the twelve powers (which segued into the writing of this book), I was ready to go back home to face my remaining responsibilities. I had been restored in strength and health.

Sometimes you need to let old foundations sweep away before you can affirm and rebuild a new way from an old self. I could not do this without the help of others. I could not do this without the help of the Holy Spirit and the sustaining help of God. This was not the first time I had been devastated by outer circumstances. It would not be the last. This time I had the mountains and God is in the mountains and God is within me.

Among the metaphysical disciples, Andrew symbolizes strength. The strength center of each of us is in the small of the back. Spiritual strength, the fruit of prayer and of meditating on strength, is born in the silence of the soul and reflected into the body at this center.

According to Fillmore:

"All strength is from God. However, each person's thoughts and actions largely determine the mold or shape into which this precious essence of strength is poured. Spiritual unfoldment and the increase of God's strength within you depends upon your determined aspirations, within and without, which are met by God's descending grace. The soul cannot buy God's strength or steal it, but rather can only open itself to it and go to meet the divine with sincere and unfailing, purposeful devotion.

"Truly, to live the spiritual life, one must be strong. One must withstand every test."

Often those on a spiritual path wonder why it is that as they grow in strength, more and more tests of strength, endurance, wisdom, and love come into their lives. It is only much later that we can see that every spiritual test leads to greater understanding and an increased capacity to be of service to the world.

We must not let ourselves be weakened by the disappointments and frustrations of human relationships. If we harbor such negativity for too long, we may even come to the point where we want to retreat or even die. Such moods cannot be allowed to weaken the spiritually minded person. By maintaining contact with the ever-renewing Spirit of infinite strength, we can be sustained by God's unfailing power and presence and can rise from disappointment and loneliness to go on, even stronger than before.

A disciplined, peaceful daily practice helps each of us to deal with the slings and arrows of outrageous fortune and strengthens us for the inner journey home. It also strengthens our physical body.

Realization of spiritual strength at the strength center, the small of the back, acts as an invigorating tonic to the silver cord—the path for the spinal life fluid that flows along the inner walls of the spinal column. Spiritual strength aids the free flow of the life fluid along the nerves and penetrates into every cell and fiber of the golden bowl—the abdominal wall that contains and supports the digestive organs. Through this process, the whole body temple is uplifted and vitalized again and again.

## ❦ Questions and Responses

Before you do the following exercise, ask yourself these questions:

As I look back on my life, what events have helped me to become a stronger person? What difficulties have I surmounted? What lessons have I learned? Can I learn new lessons now with the aid of added spiritual strength? Can I learn new lessons now in peacefulness and joy, rather than going through painful new experiences? What have I learned that I can pass on to others? How does my strength serve the world?

- Name three ways in which your past strengths have led you to new awareness.
- Name three ways in which you intend to strengthen your body, mind, emotions, or spirit in the month ahead.
- Name three ways in which your newfound strength will make a difference to the world.

## ❦ Meditation

For the meditation in silence, first follow diligently the basic meditation given in the Introduction. At the close of the exercise, connect with and realize that you are rooted in God's strength of Being. With your conscious mind, realize that the light of Spirit is descending from the spiritual center in the crown of the head. Then with the attention at the point designated as the great solar nerve center, behind the heart and stomach, repeat the invocation. Realize that you are in the presence of pure Being and immersed in Its light. As you continue, you will come into the conscious knowledge that you are wrapped in a mantle of light (pure understanding), that your feet are shod in sandals of light, and that every impulse of your soul is reaching out to express fully the Christ Consciousness within.

Next, for the special unfolding of spiritual strength, continue to allow the Presence to dwell at the center of your being.

## *Affirm*:

"I am one with the infinite strength of God."

Next, allow the Presence to drop to the small of the back and realize that the light of Spirit—which you feel but do not see—is descending from the crown of the head and organizing itself at the strength center. During this outpouring, hold steadily to this same thought:

"I am one with infinite strength."

You will feel new strength awakening within you. Next, let the Presence ascend to the power center at the root of the tongue. Then hold steadily to this thought:

"I have the power to express the sustaining strength of Spirit."

Now allow the Presence to descend to the life center, the lower part of the abdomen. There affirm:

"The pure strength of God is being expressed in and through me, and I am strengthened and sustained in all my actions."

Next, allow the Presence to return to the great center of being just back of the heart and stomach. There take up this word:

"The joy of the Lord is a wellspring within me, and I am established in divine strength."

Dwell consciously at that point, knowing that you are firmly rooted in the garden of spirituality within your own soul, that the light of Spirit is descending from the spiritual center, the crown of the head, and that new strength is flowing to every part of your whole being. The truth is that your whole body temple is the garden of God, and that every cell and fiber is made sweet and strong by this new light of the Holy Spirit. You have a strong hold on the body temple when God's presence is alive in your deepest roots, your Christ Consciousness within. Then you are more and more free to express God from the very center of your being, to bring forth the highest and the best in daily life.

Close the exercise by speaking the Lord's Prayer.

For the sake of balance, after you have finished the exercise, throw your attention for a time into the palms of the hands and tips of the fingers, also into the feet, and then even beneath the feet, realizing that you are planted on the firm foundation rock of Truth.

> *"'Be strong in the Lord, and in the strength of His might' is a great strengthening affirmation for ourselves and for others. Be steadfast, strong, and steady in thought, and you will establish strength in mind and in body. . . . Affirm yourself to be a tower of strength, within and without."*

# Chapter Three

# The Spiritual Power of Discrimination or Judgment
# Location: Pit of Stomach
# Disciple: James, Son of Zebedee

*"When we awaken to the reality of our being, the light begins to break upon us from within and we know the truth; this is the quickening of our James, or judgment, faculty. When this quickening occurs, we find ourselves discriminating between the good and the evil."*

AFFIRMATION: "The Holy Spirit is now here raising me to a consciousness of divine judgment, and the wisdom of God is expressed in all that I think, say, and do."

What does the word "judgment" mean to you? When I began to reflect in meditation on the quality of judgment, I discovered that I cannot write about the word "judgment" without writing about forgiveness. To me, the two are linked inextricably in my mind. Too often people think of judgment as something to be feared, that we are being judged by a great God in the sky who shows little mercy for even our most benign transgressions.

A friend of mine jokingly called this image the "hanging judge" syndrome. Whenever she felt tempted to judge herself unmercifully, she would realize that her mind had served up a judge who was totally implacable, that expected and demanded perfection in every area, and who was harsh and punitive. "It was only when I applied mercy to each situation that I learned to love and forgive myself and others," she told me.

Perhaps you, too, have an unyielding judge at the center of your being. This judge is composed of old mental images and erroneous convictions and conclusions. What is the solution? The solution is to apply the quality of mercy and unconditional love to that black-robed judge within you, and to forgive. Forgive the judge, forgive others, forgive yourself. Forgive every one and everything in your life. Have mercy. Begin now to dismantle old mental conditions that have led to your judgments about others, and especially about yourself. You are your own harshest critic. When you pour the balm of love upon the quality of judgment, the alchemy of that union is wisdom.

Yet it is important not to confuse judgment with discernment. We can have good judgment in our lives without judging or demeaning others. Through the process of contemplation, we can develop a keen sense of discernment—that exquisite quality that allows us to move

## The Spiritual Power of Discrimination or Judgment / 41

through life in a calmer, wiser manner, unswayed by others' criticism or condemnation. As we go through life, it is imperative to develop a keen sense of what is right or wrong for us, without judging or demeaning others. This quality of discernment helps us to make wise choices and to live more peacefully in the world. We learn the art of delicate discrimination and discernment in all that we think, say, or do.

The quality of judgment can be a great teacher when it is used *for* ourselves and others, not *against* ourselves or others. Then comes wisdom. This wisdom is symbolized by the metaphysical disciple James, just as the quality of Love is symbolized by the metaphysical disciple John. They must learn to work together in every part of your body temple.

According to Fillmore:

"The great positive and the great negative forces run through the center of our being as wisdom (judgment) in the pit of the stomach, and as love in the center of the heart. In the development of the twelve powers, these faculties are of paramount importance; they are closely related and work together in producing the strongest vibrations known to the body. In metaphysical literature James and John are called 'sons of thunder,' a title symbolizing the powerful vibrations produced by these faculties. Wisdom is a great dynamic force that carries its power to the love center. In the action and reaction between these two centers we receive our most powerful spiritual realizations. Wisdom and love, when combined, produce peace and poise, a great, dynamic spiritual center."

When we clear away old mental ideas of judgment and combine these two faculties of wisdom and love, we come into a place where we can more easily access pure ideas. Fillmore called this the process of evolving an intelligence higher than that of intellect alone. This process helps us to move toward a greater science, which he called the science of intuition and wisdom continually working through the mind. When we combine wisdom and love, we find ourselves touched and moved by the more primal energies and principles of Being. These are called pure ideas, which express themselves through the mind in the form of clear words and thoughts.

So we are moving from the old idea of judgment, both personal and erroneously punitive, to a clarity that allows us to use the faculty of divine wisdom in our work and in our lives. This is true metamorphosis.

How do you access this divine wisdom?

To access wisdom, you must consciously control and work with your body temple and the development of the mind. This ability is attained through continuous care and wise development of the twelve spiritual faculties.

What is the result of learning to live in relationship to divine wisdom and judgment? Fillmore's answer is this:

"Divine wisdom, divine judgment, has in itself the essence of profound goodness. When we really live in deep relation to divine wisdom, we shall have much greater power to combine words and actions effectively and so manifest greater wholeness and perfection in mind and body."

Who among us would not want to touch the essence of profound goodness? We are asked to live in a deep relationship with divine wisdom. That is one great purpose of practicing and incorporating these spiritual truths into our inner core self. Then comes wholeness. Then comes goodness. Then comes grace.

## ☘ Questions and Responses

Sit quietly in the silence. Place your hand over the solar plexus, the judgment center. What do you feel? What sensations, emotions, or words come to you? Ask yourself the following questions:

What does the word "judgment" mean to me? How have I judged myself in the past? How can I forgive myself for false and harsh judgments? Bring to mind all the people that you love. How have you judged them? Can you forgive yourself for judging them? Now bring to mind anyone in your life, living or dead, whom you have judged harshly. Can you forgive yourself for judging them? Can you release them and let them go? Can you pour the balm of love upon all the judgments of yourself and other people? Will you? Will you now forgive and bless all?

## ❈ Meditation

For your meditation in the silence, first take up the exercise in the Introduction, following step by step the outline given there, with the conscious mind in the front forehead fully aware of what is taking place. You will become more and more aware that the Christ Consciousness is awakening within you and that you are consciously forming new perceptive faculties not only in the front forehead but throughout your whole being, as well as calling into focus, formation, and demonstration your strong and beautiful body temple.

After you have felt a deeper realization and pervasiveness of God's presence, in you and all around you, and after you have become more deeply conscious of the flow of the Holy Spirit, continue allowing the divine Presence to dwell at the point designated as the great solar nerve center. Then take up the thought of infinite wisdom, spiritual judgment, and affirm:

"Divine wisdom is awakened within me and my soul rejoices."

Then allow the Presence to go to the judgment or wisdom center, at the pit of the stomach, and affirm that the wisdom of Almighty God is descending upon you from the spiritual center, the crown of the head, and that you are appropriating and assimilating it in the spirit of love.

Wisdom, symbolized by the metaphysical disciple

# The Spiritual Power of Discrimination or Judgment / 45

James, and love, symbolized by the metaphysical disciple John, must work together.

### *Affirm:*

"God is the name of the omnipresent wisdom in which I live, move, and have my being. Divine wisdom is awakened in me and I love to express divine judgment."

Hold this statement until your whole being is illuminated with spiritual light.

Next allow the Presence, the light of Spirit, to return to the great solar nerve center back of stomach and heart. Repeat this affirmation:

"The Presence of God transforms my fears into the spirit of power and love, and gives me a sound mind and body."

Then allow the Presence to enter the love center, the heart itself, and declare:

"I love to express the wisdom of God. My heart beats in love with the great loving heart of God. I move with greater peace, poise, and power."

Now allow the Presence to return to the great solar nerve center and speak the Lord's Prayer.

After you have finished this exercise, it is often good

to realize and affirm that your conscious mind is aware of the spiritual process going on. Then let the Presence drop down into the feet. Here realize that you are clothed in greater understanding and peace.

Remember, do not push these exercises. Practice with patience and discrimination.

This meditation may need to be repeated often for clearing and healing.

As you clear yourself of old judgments and forgive yourself and others, all the while using the spiritual affirmation exercise in this chapter, you can begin to unite the quality of love with the quality of wisdom that is developing within you. This quality of wisdom can then be applied to every area of your life so that a continuing stream of wisdom is available to you. You are devloping discernment and discrimination, coupled with forgiveness and mercy. This is a powerful spiritual combination. Thank God for all that you are learning and all insights being given to you.

*"Wisdom includes judgment, discrimination, intuition, and all the departments of mind that come under the head of knowing. The house or throne of this wise judge is at the nerve center called the solar plexus. The natural man [woman] refers to it as the pit of the stomach. The presiding intelligence at the center knows what is going on, especially in the domain of consciousness pertaining to the body and its needs. Chemistry is its specialty; it also knows all that pertains to the sensations of*

## The Spiritual Power of Discrimination or Judgment / 47

*soul and body. In its highest phase it makes union with the white light of Spirit functioning in the top brain. At the solar plexus also takes place the union between love and wisdom."*

*Chapter Four*

# The Spiritual Power of Love
# Location: Back of Heart
# Disciple: John

*"Love is the attribute that holds the soul and body together. It is the attracting force that draws our good to us according to the depth and strength of our realization of the higher energies of God's presence. The path that leads to true soul unfoldment leads to adoration of the great cause of all."*

AFFIRMATION: "The Holy Spirit is now raising me to a consciousness of divine love. I express divine love in all that I think, say, and do."

How do we learn to express the soul quality of unconditional love?

The love center is located at the back of the heart center, which is that point between the breastbone that stands as a central point of light between the higher and the lower qualities of soul expression. It is the gateway

The Spiritual Power of Love / 49

between the higher and the lower centers of spiritual power.

How do we open the gateway between the higher and the lower centers? How do we learn to walk into the very heart of love? This is no easy task. It is so far beyond our early ideas of positive thinking and positive emotions that it is as if we go from a metaphysical kindergarten into graduate school. And once this gateway is opened, there is no turning back. We are given over to love.

We have said before that positive thinking is not the same as spiritual thinking. Often people who begin a spiritual study, especially one based on metaphysical thought, believe that by merely affirming over and over whatever it is they want to happen, change, demonstrate, heal, etc., they will cause their affirmations to be answered exactly as heard. Sometimes, in the first flush of successful affirmation, (i.e., "I can get the job I want" or "I can lose twenty pounds in two months" or "this person will love me no matter what"), a terrible distortion creeps in. We begin then to feel as if we are manipulating the universe. We ask for more and more. Sometimes we receive less and less. Frustrated, we may then declare that all this metaphysical stuff just doesn't work.

When we are then tested, sometimes beyond our current capabilities, disillusionment sets in. Our positive belief systems are shattered in order that we may learn to walk into the very heart of unconditional love.

I learned this lesson through the most terrible and intense event of my life: the illness and death of my beloved son Michael. No matter how much he and I and his entire family wanted him to live, no matter how many prayers and meditations and promises made to God, Michael died. He died luminous. He died loved. He died bringing his entire family together. He died, as I have said in an earlier book, loved and healed in ways that did not concern his physical body at all.

How do you maintain your trust in a merciful and loving God when your child dies? My belief systems were shattered. I had a grudge against God. Yet somehow, even in the midst of my grief and anger, I began to see a larger purpose for Michael's life. The book I wrote about his life served to bring families together in the midst of their own tragedies. His life and his death became ultimately an act of unconditional love.

The death of my son broke my heart open. I believe that it has stayed open ever since, learning again and once again the lessons of love.

Love helped me go beyond the most devastating loss into a new awareness of how precious life is, and how much we can love the people in our lives for as long as they are here. God always leads us gently to what we need to know in order to develop and express our love and wisdom.

But we do not need tragedy in order to be loving. We do need, or so I believe, an awareness of the blessed quality of love experienced as acceptance. Acceptance of self, of others, of the flow of life and death. Acceptance of our part in God's divine plan for us. I have been helped

The Spiritual Power of Love / 51

to understand this by becoming aware of the divine feminine that Fillmore writes about so eloquently. He identifies love as "the daughter of God" and goes on to say of our continual soulwork:

> "The work can be done through individual effort, and there must always be continuous constructive action between the masculine and feminine faculties of soul and body; but the anointing with the precious love of the divine feminine is necessary to the great demonstration."

The demonstration that Fillmore is writing about is the work of the individual soul, both male and female, in opening, accessing, and using the great force of love in action in the world.

I like the fact that this founder of Unity, this old-fashioned, early-1900s philosopher, could both recognize and write about the power of the divine feminine in spiritual consciousness. In his explanation of the spiritual power of love, he quoted the following passage from Proverbs, which I have on my desk in order to inspire me to access my own divine feminine qualities:

> *"Length of days is in her right hand;*
> *And in her left hand are riches and honor.*
> *Her ways are ways of pleasantness,*
> *And all her paths are peace."*
> *(Proverbs 3:16–19, King James Version)*

But he also pointed to the quality of man's love to transform consciousness. According to Fillmore:

"In the spiritual body the love center is the heart, symbolized by the metaphysical disciple John. John loved the Master. Thus love beholds the transforming, uplifting power of the Christ Consciousness."

As we connect with the deepest part of love within us, as we desire to be more loving, more expressive, open, honest in our love, as we choose to access a greater capacity for love, we find that God meets us halfway.

"God, through love, is gently wooing us; He does not force or suppress the wild, uncultivated forces within the heart, but He gently opens avenues through which these forces may express themselves constructively and lovingly."

Each of us has wild, uncultivated places within our hearts. Stormy weather brings great passion and great intensity into our lives, which can be used to move us forward through deep and difficult times. Yet each of us longs for peacefulness and clear skies. The integration of the divine feminine and the divine masculine is a great soul task. This blending of love and intelligence within each of us, female or male, leads ultimately to a wholeness that can be expressed in loving wisdom.

How often have you heard that just by learning to love ourselves, we can be healed? While it is true that self-hatred stands in the way of expressing our true essence, self-love is only part of the equation. Love is a trinity. We can learn to love ourselves, we can extend that love to others, and we can come daily into a nourishing, loving relationship with our God.

## ✣ *Questions and Responses*

Whom do I need to accept today? Whom do I need to forgive? To whom am I willing to send love?

Here is a wonderful exercise to try every day for a month. Sit quietly and bring into your mind each person you love. Then, from your mind, send out thoughts of love and acceptance to each person. You may surround them with light as you do this. Send each person a blessing of accepting love. Then bring the image of that person from "out there," from your mind's eye picture of them surrounded by light and love, into the center of your heart. Bless and enfold each one with your love.

As you do this daily, you will be amazed at how your relationships change, and at how *you* change. Start with love toward specific individuals you deeply care about. Later, as you progress, send thoughts of love to anyone, living or dead, who harmed you or wronged you in any way. You are looking at the essence of each person, not at what he or she has done. You have surrendered judgment to the flow of love. This is a freeing exercise, and not one to be taken lightly. Its practice can often open doors within you of unhealed, unresolved issues that must be dissolved and released within you before you can go forward with an open and loving heart. You never lose by loving others. You never lose by honoring and healing your inner self. You never lose by loving God.

> "All the wild, uncultivated forces in us must be won for God, and they must be won under the law of love. Often in our frenzied, egocentric lives we forget love. Let us remember love, and let us learn to cultivate it moment by moment in our thoughts and actions. Just as John radiated love, so let us radiate it; let us feel it in our heart. Let us realize it in the very depths of our heart and then send out thoughts of love to others from that changed place within us."

## ✣ Meditation

For the meditation in the silence, first follow the outline given in the Introduction. Repeating the Lord's Prayer, with the presence of the Holy Spirit at the great nerve center at the back of the heart and stomach, give your deepest being, your indwelling Christ Consciousness, the opportunity to command, through love, the twelve faculties and to direct them in regenerative processes. Then, continuing to dwell at the point designated, take up this thought:

## The Spiritual Power of Love / 55

"I have faith in the supreme power of love."

Love and wisdom always must go hand in hand. Love alone is not enough, and needs wisdom just as wisdom needs love. Therefore, allow the light of Spirit to descend into the heart and then to the pit of the stomach, at the wisdom center. At each point hold this thought:

"Divine love and wisdom are united in me. I will sing of loving kindness and of justice."

Then allow the Presence to descend into the renunciation center, the lower end of the spinal column. Here hold this thought:

"Forgiving love cleanses, purifies, and redeems me."

Then follow the Presence to the heart center and realize that the law of love is written in your heart. Realize that in soul and body you are being made perfect through the unfolding power of divine love.

But always bear in mind that love and wisdom must find expression through the conscious mind. With your concentrated being expressing itself at the point designated as the solar nerve center, and realizing that all the windows of your soul are open toward the spiritual center (crown of the head), know and feel that the conscious mind (front forehead) is aware of your new spiritual realization and is using it freely in contact with your word;

that you are aspiring to express the love of God in all your ways; and that your spiritual realizations are shining through your eyes and are expressing themselves in your voice. Close the exercise with the Lord's Prayer, keeping the attention at the point designated as the great solar nerve center.

> *"We are here on earth, working daily to unfold soul qualities that make us always more loving, strong, pure, and more nearly perfect. We know that the body is the fruit of the soul and that as we unfold spiritual qualities within the soul, the body goes through a process of refining and uplifting. This process must continue until we demonstrate a body fashioned after the pattern of the body of light."*

# Chapter Five

# The Spiritual Power of Power
# Location: Root of Tongue
# Disciple: Philip

*"Then do not fear to develop your power and mastery. They are not to be exercised on other people, but on yourself."*

AFFIRMATION: "The Holy Spirit is now here raising me to a consciousness of divine power, and I am established in the mastery and dominion of Spirit."

Power! What a misunderstood word. One so fraught with the idea of force over others that many women and men on a spiritual path run away from the very word itself, as if it were somehow "not spiritual" to ask for, develop, attain, and use power. Women in our culture are especially trained not to become powerful, as if in so doing, they will make others less by making themselves more. But power is not about more. It is about the development of strength, competence, confidence, creativity, intelligence. It requires accessing our own innate capacities in order to bring those qualities out into the world with a dynamic clarity. Power has no gender. It is a creative force to serve the world.

On a spiritual path, we seek power over ourselves, over the little, frightened, weak, error-prone self that longs to be firm and strong and clear and wise. This struggle between the lower and the higher self can go on for decades. In truth, we are as powerful as our intention and beliefs. Changing a powerless belief system to one of power, of empowerment, of effective and dynamic personal and spiritual leadership is an awesome and ongoing task.

We do not put on power as if we are putting on a power suit. In fact, an industrious clearing away of old thought forms and erroneous thinking, coupled with a firm desire to be of service to the world, is a vital step in accessing and developing our spiritual power.

The expression of power in each of us is regulated by our thoughts, our words, and our actions. The metaphysical disciple Philip symbolizes power. Power expresses itself through soul and body and mind at the point in the throat where the hypoglossus muscle is located. Metaphysicians call this place in the throat the power center. Power operates through the nerve aggregations in the throat that control the larynx. The thyroid gland is a part of, and is directly connected with, the power center.

The power center may be compared to the amplifying or stepping-up device of a radio. The audio amplifier in a receiving set simply increases the power of the voice of the singer or speaker until his or her words may be heard at great distance. In the human organism, the life current is harnessed by the power center, where it comes under control of each person's deepest being and is then spoken into expression or is intelligently directed to its work in soul, mind, and body.

According to Fillmore:

> "The power center in the throat controls all the vibratory energies of the organism. It is the open door between the formless and the formed worlds of vibrations pertaining to the expression of sound. Every word that goes forth receives its specific character from the power faculty."

Every one of you who reads this book should begin now to look at all the ways in which you are powerful. Have you come out of poverty to educate yourself and do good work in the world? You are powerful. Have you raised children, loved well, taken care of others with grace and courage? You are powerful. Are you an artist, shaping your creations through words on paper, paint, dance, or another medium of expression? As you shape something beautiful out of nothing but an amorphous desire to express yourself and to give to others through that creative expression, you are indeed powerful. Do you serve through business, through sport, through teaching, through counseling, through any and all positive, life-affirming activities in the world around you? Do you change the world around you by your presence, by your work, by your passion? You are indeed powerful.

## ❧ Questions and Responses

- Name three ways in which you give your power away.
- Name three areas of your life in which you intend to be more powerful.
- Name three areas of your life where you feel empowered.
- Name three things you can do in order to become more spiritually powerful.

Place your hand on the spiritual power center, at the base of the throat where the thyroid is located. Speak words of encouragement, praise and acceptance to this center. Ask for increased communication, clarity, energy. Ask to be of service in the world. Listen to what the power center has to say to you.

## ❧ Meditation

The thyroid gland, located across the front of the throat, was the first of the ductless glands to begin to yield its secrets to science. Added power and control are

## The Spiritual Power of Power / 61

felt throughout the whole body temple by allowing the Presence, the light of Spirit, to descend from the spiritual center in the crown of the head down to the thyroid gland and into the base of the neck. After so doing, you will realize that the all-knowing power of God's word is being poured out from on high at these very points. Your whole being will begin to become illumined. Be careful, however, not to overextend yourself in this exercise at first, and never carry out such an exercise except in the spirit of selfless love.

For the meditation in the silence, first follow the outline given in the Introduction. Experience the realization of the outpicturing of the Holy Spirit throughout your whole being. Continuing to hold the attention at the great solar nerve center, affirm:

"God's power is being given to me in mind and in body."

Then allow the Presence to ascend to the base of the neck, including the whole throat, and even the tip of the tongue. Realize that the light is pouring out upon you from the spiritual center in the crown of the head, and that you have the power to appropriate and assimilate this light. This is a good word to hold:

"Your name is Spirit. I know You as the one, all-powerful, all-knowing Mind, now giving me full control of the powers of being."

Then allowing the Presence, the Holy Spirit, to descend to the heart, meditate upon the power of divine love. Dedicate your realization of power to the loving service of God. Holding the attention at the heart center, take up this prayer:

> "I am humble and receptive in heart. God expresses Himself in me and through me in love and power."

Next allow the Presence to descend into the lower part of the abdomen, the life center, with this thought:

> "God's purity is awakened in me. Power from God raises me to a higher consciousness and realization."

Again allow the Presence to ascend to the point named the great solar nerve center, and affirm:

> "I am rooted in the peace, poise, and power of God. Through me, God is doing His work in love and wisdom, and I rejoice and am thankful for the good that I can do through Him."

Close the drill by softly repeating the Lord's Prayer. During the whole drill, be sure that the conscious mind in the front forehead is feeling the new power that you are generating. This tends to remold your perceptive powers more and more after the divine pattern. After the exercise, sit for a few moments, first with the attention in the palms of the hands and fingertips, and then in the feet and beneath the feet.

May the words work powerfully within you!

*"The Holy Spirit is God in action, and the activity of Spirit gives us power. It is a force generating from God that meets our strongest aspirations and enables us to move out to others by our thoughts, words, and actions."*

## Chapter Six

# The Spiritual Power of Imagination
# Location: Between the Eyes
# Disciple: Bartholomew

*"When the faculties of the mind are understood in their threefold relation—spirit, soul, body—it will be found that every form and shape originated in the imagination. It is through the imagination that the formless takes form."*

AFFIRMATION: "The Holy Spirit is now here raising me to a consciousness of divine imagination, and I see greater spiritual perfection everywhere."

For many years, I have awakened before dawn and gone outside to wait for the light. Weather permitting, I can sit on a bench on my terrace or stand in the corner of the eaves, and wait and watch for the light to come over the mountains and through the trees and into my mind and heart. This is not a time for asking. It is a time for listening. It is a time for receiving. Recently I read about the time called "forelight," that time before dawn when the world is very quiet and still and pregnant with possibilities. It is a time for allowing fertile ideas to stir, to awaken, to come to the forefront of our consciousness. It is a time of latent creativity.

As I wait for the sun to break over the horizon, I cup my hands. I want to receive the light. I can feel it first on my forehead when sunrise soars over the tops of the trees and touches me there. It is a palpable feeling, to be touched by light in the exact place where the centers of Understanding and Will sit between my brows, there where the mystical third eye is said by the ancients to awaken each of us to our true task. The sun falls on the top of my head too, where the twin powers of imagination and faith reside. I can feel it as a benediction. I have to close my eyes against the sun then, for it is so bright, so strong, so warm. But even with eyes closed, I can feel its power penetrating into every cell of my body. Preparing me for the day ahead. When for some reason I miss this sunrise encounter with the light, I work less well.

The center of imagination is called "the visioning faculty." Jesus' apostle Bartholomew symbolizes the faculty of divine imagination. Between the eyes is a ganglionic nerve center which, when spiritually quickened, will set the divine imaging power into operation. While it may appear in the diagram of the twelve powers that the power of divine imagination resides in the back of the head, according to Fillmore it begins at the third eye point between the brows and continues through to the back of the head.

This visioning faculty, when awakened, has the power to engrave new pictures, new possibilities, within every cell of our bodies. The very word "character" has at its root the word "engrave." So we engrave our character through the process of prayerful visioning of the good, the true, and the beautiful.

Imagination is also an interpreter of symbols. It is a magnet. It magnetizes and attracts to us what we truly desire. We must learn to get the picture clear, and then keep the focus adjusted. Imagination is the formative power of thought. Its first command is: "Let there be light." It helps us to translate the light into thought, action, and manifestation. Divine imagination is the chisel used to mold the kingdom within.

As a writer, I use imagination daily. My soul quickens and thrills to the inspiring words offered by Fillmore to explain, with spiritual authority, the processes by which envisioning turns into concrete, palpable reality.

I remember asking years ago, when I wrote down my deepest dreams, to write "books that served the world." I saw a woman with her arms outstretched to the sky, rising out of an open book. Years later, through a series of challenging and unlikely circumstances, I owned a small publishing company in California that specialized in books that helped people deal with caregiving, loss, and death. Its logo was: "Books to serve the world." On the spine of each book was the figure of a woman, arms outstretched to the sky, rising out of the pages of an open book.

The Spiritual Power of Imagination / 67

While the publishing company no longer exists, I did continue to write a number of books, which, I devoutly hope, serve the world.

That original image became an integral part of me. It was envisioned by spirit, given to me as a gift of spirit, and brought into manifestation by my mental, emotional, and physical concentration on making that dream a reality. Forms are always manifestations of ideas.

According to Fillmore:

"Spirit imparts its ideas through a universal language. Instead of being explained by words and phrases as used in ordinary language, the idea is formed and projected in its original character. This system of transferring intelligence is called symbolism. It is the only universal and correct means of communicating ideas."

The woman rising out of the open pages of a book became an archetype, a mythical symbol for me to express my creativity in the world. It serves me well.

Yet you do not have to be a writer or any other type of creative artist in order to explore your own symbols and your own imaging faculty. We do it all the time. When we really look at the imaging faculty and its spiritual power, we realize that all structures are thought concentrations.

Our imaging faculty is quite powerful, and the thought forms we create in consciousness have a great effect in our life. We are always manifesting in the outer world that which takes place in our inner thought realm.

According to Fillmore:

> "The imagination has its center of action directly between the eyes. This is the point of expression for a set of tissues that extend back into the brain and connect with an imaging or picture-making function near the root of the optic nerve. Through this faculty you can project an image of things that are without, or ideas that are within."

I have often wondered how a man like Fillmore, coming out of a traditional Midwestern upbringing in the 1800s, could found a spiritual movement in 1889 that has extended to the present day. Millions of readers all over the world find inspiration in his teachings through *Daily Word*, and other hundreds of thousands of students read his books and take part in Unity classes, churches, and retreats. This was a man who was inspired by other philosophical teachings, especially those of Emerson, and who exemplified in his life Christian mysticism renewed and brought to life through practical spirituality. When I read the following passage, I understood why his teachings endure.

> "When the imagination is subjective and spiritual and the will and the understanding are objective and alert, we have the creative artist. Then the

understanding develops its greatest freedom and originality. It is no longer bound by the traditions of the past in literature, art, music, drama, science or religion, but launches out into the deep and brings up the 'pearl of great price,' original creative genius and life."

He contrasted this type of inspired writing with a purely intellectual approach to information.

"Very intellectual people, concentrating the intensity of their thought in the head, fail to connect with the substance, life, and love centers in the body, and their work, although it may be very brilliant, lacks what we term 'soul.' The thought creations of this type seldom live long. Where the thought form and its substance are evenly balanced, the projected idea endures indefinitely."

As a writer, I have been inspired and instructed by the twelve powers that Fillmore identified. He even helped me to see dreams as messengers of truth, a valuable tool for anyone to use in whatever type of endeavor. You can use the following passage nightly before you go to sleep, in order to access what Spirit is trying to teach.

According to Fillmore:

"There is a scientific law behind every dream, every vision: Everything that happens in the outer world first takes place in the inner realm of thought. The inner realm of thought is where the Spirit of Truth operates to manifest itself in the outer. Often when we become still, as in sleep, the Spirit of Truth throws messages onto the screen of our mind. These messages are thought pictures, and are called 'dreams' by the recipient. We can learn to read the thought pictures in order to receive the messages they bring to us. If we take our thoughts to the center of imagination within, holding to the purpose of realization for light and wisdom, the power of Spirit will clarify the Truth.

"Divine imagination, an instrument in the hands of the Spirit of Truth, manifesting through mental pictures and images, is often prophetic. We read the symbols of our thought, in silent meditation, to discern what manifestations we are creating through our thought."

Imagine being able to read every thought symbol that comes to us, not only in our dreams, but in the imaginative symbolism of our waking thoughts as well, and so be guided by our divine imagination to make wise choices and to create well.

Imagination is much more than idle visual pictures thrown upon the screen of the mind.

Ultimately, imagination is an attribute of God. It is the formative power of thought, the molding powers of the mind. It is what gives shape, tone, color to thinking. Every word or every combination of words has an image behind it—a thought picture.

The Spiritual Power of Imagination / 71

We all have free access to God; therefore, we have free access to His imagination. This is divine imagination. Do you desire to be strong, healthy, wise, and lovable? Imagine and reimagine yourself to be all good things. Touch the divine creative faculty of imagination within yourself, and you will manifest exactly what you image.

## ✣ Questions and Responses

- Name three things in your life that you want to imagine into being.
- Name three things in your life that you want to reimagine—that is, undo, redo, adjust, or release.

    Look at your life from the perspective of spiritual imagination. Do you have stalled projects, something left unfinished when the initial enthusiam of the imagination faltered? How can you resurrect the power of your envisioning faculty in order to complete this project?
- Name a deep dream of yours that is yet to be realized. How can you use the imaging faculty to breathe new life into that dream? Are you willing to do this?

## ⚜ Meditation

For this meditation in the silence, first take up the exercise given in the Introduction. When repeating the invocation there, realize that you are "in the presence of pure Being" and that you are "immersed in the Holy Spirit of life, love, and wisdom." Try to feel and see with your inner eye the deeper you. Allowing the Presence to dwell at a point back of the heart, realize this prayer:

"The image of the Christ Consciousness is implanted within me."

Realize that the quickening power of the word is bringing that divine image into manifestation. Then allow the Presence, the light of Spirit, to ascend into the seat of the imaging faculty, between the eyes, realizing this word:

"I am the image and likeness of God Consciousness in manifestation."

Allowing the Presence to drop down to the heart center, affirm:

"My heart is beating in perfect accord with the great heart of God. Through the eyes of love I behold everyone and everything as pure and perfect."

The Spiritual Power of Imagination / 73

Next allow the Presence to drop down into the feet. Then affirm:

"I am able to stand straight before God; I am walking in perfect accord with Him."

Then quietly let the Presence take up its abode at the back of the heart. Let men and women hold this prayer:

"I am created in the image and likeness of God."

Then close the exercise with the Lord's Prayer. In conclusion, as in the previous exercises, drop the attention down into the feet, and let it dwell there for a while. By this time you will have discovered that by so doing you set into activity all the spiritual powers of your being.

*"It is through divine imagination that the soul first gets the impulse to expand. In the silence we learn to extend our vision beyond things as they appear temporarily. We do not ignore the conditions that face us, but we look through them to what they can become. As our goal is greater light and purity, so we must first go through many periods of constant pruning. The soul must face its challenges yet somehow always see these 'in the light.' Imagination means seeing the wholeness and purpose in each condition and challenge. By blessing our situation as we face it, we help to bring about*

*healing, and eventual overcoming will be ours. Imagination leads us to the realization that at the center of all life there is a perfect pattern, something which cannot be improved or disputed, the image of God, and that when we see through eyes of spiritual imagination, we see through the eyes of God."*

# Chapter Seven

# The Spiritual Power of Understanding
## Location: Front Brain
## Disciple: Thomas

*"Spiritual understanding is developed in the feminine realm of the soul."*

AFFIRMATION: "The Holy Spirit is now here, raising me to a consciousness of divine understanding. I am inspired."

"Make your mind a lighted lamp." I remember a Unity teacher telling me this years ago, as I struggled to come to a better understanding of spiritual principles and universal laws.

I believe that the soul quality of spiritual understanding can, when developed properly, lead the sincere meditator to a life of clarity and discernment. This understanding is symbolized in the twelve powers at a power point located in the front brain and connected by the twin faculty of divine will, which is located right above the point of power known as divine understanding.

Understanding and will, once united, form the basis for wisdom. This is not an everyday knowingness, nor just the wisdom of age or experience. The experiences of your life are great teachers that lead you to deeper understanding. I believe that most people learn through an emotional personal connection, and only later can apply reason and logic to the seemingly inexplicable challenges that come to all of us. But life is not all about challenges. If you look back on a life well lived, you will see that courage, abundance, peace, wisdom, health, and love walked hand in hand with you even in the midst of the greatest difficulties.

The basis of Unity teachings is that you can work through the difficult times through the application of spiritual law. This is not to guarantee a life full of blue skies and sunshine all the time. But as you walk through personal storms, you have the ability not only to survive, but to go on stronger and wiser than before, and at the same time, as you continually access the light within, the twelve spiritual powers walk hand in hand with you.

I have known people who are full of a wise sweetness that spills over to all those around them. As they surmounted personal challenges, they became the good that they sought. There is an old adage in metaphysics that states, "If you are looking for water, you must become the water." If you are looking for clarity, understanding, abundance, wisdom, love, etc., you find it by accessing the truth of yourself within, not in looking to the external to provide you with outer qualities. The cosmic irony in all of this is that as you "become the water," "become the light," become whatever you desire to be from the inside out, the external world then begins to mirror back to you a changed condition. You find more tenderness, more gentleness, more mercy and loving kindness in the world. You find more peace around you as you develop a core self that contains peace of mind within its parameters. As you change, your world will change.

Thomas is the disciple that Fillmore designates as the metaphysical representation of divine understanding. Who better than a doubter, one who questions, one who asks to be shown, irrefutably, what is true and what is false?

When I am faced with situations in my life that I cannot seem to change, when I feel dim and foggy and despairing, I often take long walks to clear my head. During these walks I will contact that point of divine understanding within my front forehead and ask this question: "What is the truth of this situtation?" Again and again I will ask the question, until clarity flares up and illuminates the corners of my mind.

When you make your mind a lighted lamp, when you access the energy contained within the spiritual point between the eyes known as divine understanding, you will begin to see things "in the light." You will begin to perceive the truth of each situation as it presents itself in your life. You will begin to walk in wisdom, with the twin points of divine understanding and divine will as a compass light to guide you on your way.

According to Fillmore:

> "Divine understanding is the perceiving power of the mind; it is often called the eye of the will. Divine will is the governing, directing power of mind. These twin spiritual faculties operate through the front brain. Working together, they penetrate into the invisible realm of thought to direct and bring forth the light and inspiration of Divine Mind. They connect the inner world of thought with the outer world of manifestation."

There are many times when the understanding faculty is obscured, when it seems to operate in dim light. This is part of the process of spiritual unfoldment. But within each of us is the spiritual light to understand, and we may strengthen the faculty of understanding by making powerful affirmations. When the consciousness is lit with spiritual understanding, it is able to demonstrate the attributes of God and to understand the work of Spirit in the physical world. This understanding gives clear insight and inspiration to the will faculty.

Although you may be sincere in resolving to demonstrate a better life for yourself, old and limited mental conceptions are often barriers to a new, unlimited understanding. This causes resistance, which Fillmore called "a letting down in consciousnesss." It takes patient, persistent, creative thought to remold the perceptive and directive powers of the mind. While the process may seem slow and endless, the rewards will come when our intent

The Spiritual Power of Understanding / 79

is to appropriate enough energy to activate love and wisdom in our lives. With persistence, the pure light within us will enable us to arouse sufficient life energy and love within to lift up the whole consciousness. Then we will perceive with an understanding heart and see with understanding eyes as we radiate wisdom from the inner realms into our outer lives.

Ask yourself often, "What is the truth of this situation?" Ask daily, hourly in the midst of crisis, for the light of divine understanding to beam upon the situation or problem that needs resolution. Ask for discernment and wisdom. Ask that your spiritual understanding be united with divine will. Ask for the light of divine understanding and it will be given to you.

## ❖ Questions and Responses

- Name three areas in your life that need to be changed for the better. Ask yourself, "What is the truth of this situation?" Write down your responses.
- Pick one area to clear up by asking for divine light and understanding to help you. When your problem or difficulty is solved, tackle the next one.
- Continue to clear up your life, step by step. If something seems insurmountable or out of your control, leave that challenge alone for a while and go back to it later as you grow in increased understanding. It may change in the meantime.
- Name three areas in your life that are wonderful. If

you cannot think of three areas in your life that are working well, shine the light of divine understanding upon three important areas and "become the light." Become the joy, peace, love, goodness, etc., that you want. Continue daily until you feel the change within you.
- Ask yourself, "Am I willing to let go of this problem? Am I willing for things to be different? Am I willing to be more conscious of the choices I make in my life? Am I willing to understand? Am I willing to change?" Write down your responses.

## ✣ Meditation

For a regenerative meditation in the silence, begin with the exercise in the Introduction. Continue to allow the Presence to dwell at the solar nerve center and declare that your body temple is the garden of God, that the indwelling Christ Consciousness in action is standing in the midst of you, directing and controlling the ebb and flow of your spiritual energies. Hold this thought:

> "The Christ Consciousness of God is active in me; the breath of God gives me understanding. I am transformed by the renewal of my mind."

Now allow the Presence to ascend to the front brain, to the center of the faculties of understanding and will. Here meditate on this thought:

"Divine understanding is awakened in me, and I am divinely guided in all that I do. I see spiritually, feel spiritually, know spiritually, and act spiritually."

Now allow the Presence to drop down into the feet, holding this thought:

"My feet are placed on the firm rock of divine understanding. I am shod in sandals of pure gold. I am governed, guided, and directed by the wisdom and power of the indwelling Christ Consciousness."

The feet represent the understanding and guiding power that contacts materiality, the outer world.

Next allow the Presence to rise to the point at the back of the heart and stomach. Feel the spiritual flow of thought from head to foot. Realize again that your whole body is the garden of God, that every spiritual center in this garden is imbued with the perfect light of Christ Consciousness.

Close the exercise by repeating the Lord's Prayer. The Christ Consciousness of God in the midst of you is mighty to heal, to guide, to uplift you, bodily and mentally. By this time you have discovered that the unfolding of your spiritual faculties cannot be pushed.

The work that you are doing now elicits deep responses from within your core self. It is wise to take some time now in order to assimilate and integrate the changes that are taking place within you. The next spiritual quality, that of divine will, is so powerful that the system needs to stabilize before it leaps forward into new spiritual energy. Fillmore asked that the student pause after accessing and working with the quality of divine understanding.

He said:

"The earnest student may become aware of some barriers to further development. It is sometimes best to cease the exercises for a time in order to digest the inspiraton which has already been received. When you are again centered in the new light, well poised, you will be guided back to the exercises for continuation of this pure work."

This book is not to be read in one sitting. It is to be used again and again as you progress in spiritual understanding. The spiritual powers yet to come—those of divine will, divine order, divine zeal, divine renunciation and elimination, and divine generative life—will set you on a new course after the previous spiritual qualities of divine faith, divine strength, divine discrimination or judgment, divine love, divine power, divine imagination, and divine understanding have been practiced prayerfully for some time in order to integrate their qualities within your inner core self.

*"No one ever attained spiritual consciousness without striving for it. The first step is to ask. . . . Prayer is one form of asking, seeking, and knock-*

ing. Then make your mind receptive to the higher understanding, through silent meditations and affirmations of Truth. The earnest desire to understand spiritual things will open the way, and revelation within and without will follow."

*Chapter Eight*

# The Spiritual Power of Will
# Location: Center Front Brain
# Disciple: Matthew

*"This acquirement of a knowledge of the divine will is not the work of an instant; it results from patient and persistent spiritual study, prayer, and meditation."*

AFFIRMATION: "The Holy Spirit is now here raising me to a consciousness of divine will. I am willing to do His will."

As we look outside ourselves and see how we are seemingly powerless over certain events in the world, how we cannot protect our loved ones from death, we may despair.

How can we know when to use the strong developed power of executive will, the focused, determined strength that we have developed as a response to life's challenges, and when to surrender, let go, let God? When is our personal will insufficient and the only remedy is "Thy will be done?"

I learned this lesson when my mother lay dying.

She died inch by inch, day by day, week by week, month by month, year by year. I could not save her from the slow disintegration of her faculties. I could not save her from dementia or paralysis. I could not speed her progress into God's arms. I could not keep her safe and well. I anguished over this for seven years. I had no power over her or her journey. My will could not supersede her soul's lessons.

What I did come to discover was my own strength of will in the midst of unending, interminable crisis. My power of will lay in being able to show up for her, day by day, month by month, year by year. Show up and serve. Show up and encourage. Show up and love. Often I was tired, harried, overly busy, depressed, preoccupied with my own concerns, anguished at the evidence of all that she was suffering. But I did it. I showed up. I loved her through it. Perhaps that is not a big thing. Women have been doing this for millennia, and many men as well, but it was an enormous task for me. It was an ongoing test of character, patience, courage, and love. It was a test of will. And in the midst of this seemingly hopeless situation, I found a quiet power within myself that sustained me throughout the seven years of my mother's illness, and throughout the last three weeks of her dying.

There are no medals for standing by and watching a loved one die. There should be.

When it came to my mother's last weeks on earth, I had to let go of all my assumptions about strength and power and will. I had to turn 180 degrees and say a thousand times a day, "Not my will, but Thine be done." Over the seven years of my mother's illness, I moved back and forth in a strange dance of will. I surrendered her care to God, yet again and again I took back the reins of her care and took charge. My sisters were with me the last few weeks of my mother's death. (One sister had helped me with her care for years.) Each of us brought to our mother's bedside all of our own will, all of our own assumptions and perceptions of how and when she should die. We each had our own pictures of her passing.

A remarkable synergy developed over those last weeks of shared caring. Each of us surrendered our will to God's will. Each of us surrendered our mother in love. Each of us was strong and loving in her own way, although we came from three different religious traditions, and led three very different lives. Finally my mother, whose own indomitable will to live was amazing, let go and let God take her home. We three sisters were there at her bedside, holding hands, when she took her last quiet breath. It is a scene I will never forget.

The power of our own will, when properly and prayerfully developed and sustained over decades, is remarkable. It is composed of all that we have learned—all our discipline, our desire, our capacity to grow and to serve well in the world. Yet when it is time to learn a new lesson—that of surrender, that of God's will, not mine, be done—we are brought to our knees. It is the opposite of all that we have learned, and only discernment will instruct us as to whether we are giving up and giving in to another's will, or if, indeed, we are guided and directed by God's will.

This surrender does not come easily, nor all at once. It is developed in quietness and in trust. God does not ask us to become weak-willed, wishy-washy, unfocused, undisciplined. No. The personal empowerment and strength we have developed will stand us in good stead. We do not go backward by surrendering to God's will. On the contrary. When all that we have tried to do on our own is not working, when we meet closed doors, we then remember that the door to the soul opens inward. We trust enough to acquiesce to a higher power and another way of being in the world. We access and add to our own qualities of will the awesome and tender power of God's will.

How will we know when to surrender? We will know. The more we are attuned to the still small voice within, the more we can indeed "let go and let God" when harsh lessons come into our lives. And when the crisis has passed, God's will is still there, as well as God's care. We will be living in God's will and under the shelter of almighty arms. We will find ourselves strengthened then for the rest of the journey. We will walk in Grace.

According to Fillmore:

"Too often we are involved in external entanglements and confusion so that our consciousness has lost the real central power of Spirit. At such times we are more self-willful than God-willful. This is the cause of our suffering. We have lost almost all conception of what it is to hear and to heed the voice of the indwelling Christ Consciousness. . . .

"The devout soul is willing that the will of God shall be done within, but may be uncertain as to the way. We do more than merely repeat a prayer; we must realize it in the very depths of our heart until our every faculty and our every cell responds. A good prayer for guidance is this:

" 'I am guided, governed, and directed by the wisdom and power of my indwelling Christ Consciousness. All my ways are pleasant and all my paths are peaceful.' "

This realization opens the way so that the light of Spirit may descend from the higher realms of the mind and establish itself within the soul.

Divine will is the mediator between God and each human being. It operates between the inner realms of mind and the outer manifestation.

Matthew, the metaphysical disciple, symbolizes the will, the executive power of the mind. Divine will together with its twin faculty of divine understanding (as symbolized by Thomas), operates in the forehead, the front brain. Every high spiritual realization, whether it is a realization of love, of power, or of health—should be gently brought to the attention of these twin faculties so they may complete the connection between the invisible world of thought and the outer world of manifestation.

One of the most powerful affirmations we can make is to know that "divine will is good will."

Then we can trust and trust again, through every spiritual test that comes our way.

## ✲Questions and Responses

- Name three times in which you have followed your own will, regardless of the still small voice from within. What was the result?
- Name three times in which you have given your power over to another's will. What was the result?
- Identify an area in your life that needs divine will. Are you willing to "let go and let God" take over? If not, when do you think you would be willing to relinquish your personal will to divine will?
- Practice saying, "Thy will be done," each time a difficulty comes into your mind.
- Take each problem now and lay it on the altar of God's will. Are you willing to surrender your problems to God? Are you willing to trust in divine will? If not now, when?

## ✲Meditation

A meditation for the silence is to go within and take up the exercise given in the Introduction. Then, allowing the Presence to continue to dwell at the back of the heart and stomach, at the point designated as the great solar nerve center, realize that God and God's laws are all.

Then allow the Presence to ascend to the front forehead, center of the twin faculties of will and understanding, and affirm:

> "I am conscious of the will of God. I am glorified in understanding."

Next allow the Presence to drop down into the order center, at the back of the navel, and affirm:

> "My understanding is open. My will is alert. I am living the law of good."

Gradually you will come to know that God's loving, sheltering will is within you and about you, and this realization will give you a deeper consciousness of security and understanding. Once again, allow the Presence to ascend to the point designated as the great central sun, and close the exercise by softly repeating the Lord's Prayer.

In conclusion, for the sake of perfect balance, throw the attention down into the feet and know that the will of God, working in your greater understanding of divine law, is working within you. The feet represent that part of the body that contacts the earth, and also the affairs of the world. Therefore, it is necessary always to come back in consciousness to a grounded place of equilibrium and poise.

> *"Stubborn, willful, resistant states of mind congest the life flow; they are followed by cramps and congestion. The will often compels the use of the various organs of the body beyond their normal capacity, and the results are found in strained nerves and strained muscles and in impaired sight and impaired hearing... The remedy is daily relaxation, meditation, prayer."*

## Chapter Nine

# The Spiritual Power of Order
# Location: Navel
# Disciple: James, Son of Alphaeus

*"The divine law of order working in the subconsciousness unearths buried talents, reveals hidden powers, and paves the way for their expression. The divine law of order coordinates the mind powers so that new inspirations may come forth unhindered. The divine law of order emphasizes the overcoming power, thereby abolishing our fear and despair. While we are apparently undergoing continual change, both physically and mentally, the changeless law of order is operating in the spiritual depths of each being."*

AFFIRMATION: "The Holy Spirit is now here raising me to a consciousness of divine order, and I realize that the law of God is fulfilled in me."

When I first began to write this book, I thought it would be an easy task. What better use of words and ideas than to take the spiritual philosophy of a great metaphysical teacher, and bring those words and ideas into a new century? Yet when I began to prayerfully compose my own ideas and words into a coherent whole, I found that I had far to go in learning and using the twelve powers that Fillmore wrote about so eloquently in the early 1900s. Only by appropriating the very spirit of each of the twelve powers was I able to move forward.

I had always used the principle of divine order. I used it to bring order out of chaos in every situation. I used it to clear away nonloving and idle states of mind. I used it to give away, clear away, clean up, move on, and start over again and again in my life. Applying divine order was essential in order for me to accomplish anything worthwhile.

Yet when I began to write this book, I found that my own ideas of how it should be presented had to give way to a higher order. Instead of highly structured, reasoned pages (which I wished for), I found that deeper levels of spirit were working within me to create the book in a new way. It became a mosaic, as if I were lovingly putting together a stained glass window. It became an exercise in patience and in prayer. The more I asked for divine order and spiritual understanding concerning this book, the more I had to sweep away earlier pages, both mine and Fillmore's, and reassemble the building blocks of words into a new order. A divine order. This process taught me a great deal. It is teaching me still.

It seems to me that all of life is a continual striving for divine order. A continual letting go of the old, including even the old cells of the body, as we grow daily in understanding. A continual letting go of old erroneous perceptions, in order to give way to new clarity. A letting go of people, places, and things, in order to make way for our soul's desires.

To speak the word of divine order in every situation, and through constant change in our lives, is a way toward a still point of wholeness in the midst of chaos. We may speak the word originally out of a divine disatisfaction with our lives as they are right now. We then set into motion a spiritual chain of events that leads us both deeper to our inner spiritual core of order, and also wider and higher, to expanded perceptions.

If you dare, begin to speak the words "divine order" as you bring into your mind every part of your life and affairs that you are dissatisfied with. Place your hand on the order center at the pit of your stomach as you declare the word of divine order for your body. Use the words "divine order" as you clean up your desk, clear out your closets, balance your checkbook. Whisper the words "divine order" as you prayerfully examine your relationships. Declare the words "divine order" as you face a mountain of work. Use the words "divine order" as a sweeping mantra, one that lifts you out of what does not work, and into a new sweetness and clarity and simplicity. Ask again and again that your mind, body, and ideas show forth God's perfect order. Divine order is mind, idea, and then manifestation.

According to Fillmore:

"The metaphysical disciple James (son of Alphaeus) represents law and order. His work was to cooperate with the other disciples, just as the orderly movement of a play depends upon the cooperation of the players. The center of order in the body is located at a nerve center at the back of the navel. By employing prayer and meditation, one may quicken the ganglionic nerve cells at the order center. It is through the navel that the unborn baby receives sustenance from its mother; so it is through this order center that the soul, spiritually quickened, receives the divine nourishment direct from the Father–Mother–God. Through our meditation and consecration the spiritual laws are unfolded to us from within."

Since every inner realization corresponds with an outer manifestation, by speaking the words "divine order" into every area of our lives, we encourage divine order to radiate its power into the other faculties and set them into sustained activity.

## ✤ Questions and Responses

- Take a look around each room in your house, or your office. What needs to be rearranged, cleared, disposed of? What can you do to bring divine order and harmony into your space?

- Next take each piece of your life and examine it. What is required to bring your life into more harmonious order? Examine your attitudes, your prejudices, your preferences. Without judging, take each to the light and ask for divine order and clarity to fill your mind so that you can be more discerning. Look carefully at your habits. Do not judge yourself. Simply ask for divine order and harmony within your body temple and within your emotional center.
- Then carefully, slowly, prayerfully, begin to bring change into your life, one step at a time. When things get stirred up, go back to the point of divine order in your stomach and declare the words "divine order" until you are calm again. Do not try to control situations or people as they change. Simply declare divine order and let the changes work their way through your life. Return often to the still point within. Divine order is your spiritual key.

## ❋ Meditation

For the regenerative meditation in the silence, first take up the exercise given in the Introduction. Continuing to allow the Presence to dwell at the point designated as the great central sun, at the back of the heart and stomach, affirm:

> "Divine order is becoming active in my mind, body, and affairs, and all things are working together for my good."

Realize that, under divine law, the rule of infinite mind is awakened in you and that every function and organ of your being is inspired with health, harmony, peace, joy, and satisfaction.

Then let the Presence descend to the order center at the back of the navel, and affirm:

> "The law of the spirit of life creates and realizes divine order in my life."

As you dwell upon this powerful statement, realize that the light of Spirit from on high, from the spiritual center in the crown of the head, is descending upon you, and that you are laying hold of a new understanding of the divine law of life. Next allow the Presence to center in the small of the back, the strength center. Then, more perfectly relaxed in mind and body, affirm:

> "The law of divine order and harmony is satisfied in me, and I behold myself a tower of spiritual strength and stability."

Then let the Presence ascend to the power center at the root of the tongue and the base of the neck, and realize:

"I am connected to the power that sets into activity God's perfect law; every function of my mind, every organ of my body, is working in divine order."

Next let the light of Spirit return to the order center at the back of the navel, and declare:

"Praise God, the law of divine order is satisfied in me, and I am at peace with all mankind."

Then, allow the Presence to return to the point designated as the great central sun. There realize that the laws of God are written in your heart and that your delight is to direct your life according to His laws. Close the exercise by softly repeating the Lord's Prayer.

After the drill is ended, throw the attention down into the feet; and declare that your house is in order and that all the forces of your being are working to glorify God.

*" . . . There must be a conscious physical change before the complete demonstration in mind and body is manifest. Thoughts work themselves out in things, and we get the full result of their work only when we follow them consciously every step of the way and help them along. Watch your thoughts as they work their way through your organism, and if you find that some pure thought of spiritual life is striving to free the life in the appetites and passions . . . help it by consciously elevating that life to the open door of your mind."*

# Chapter Ten

# The Spiritual Power of Zeal
# Location: Back of the Head, Medulla
# Disciple: Simon the Canaanite

*"Energy is zeal in motion, and energy is the forerunner of every effect."*

AFFIRMATION: "The Holy Spirit is now here raising me to a consciousness of divine zeal. I enthusiastically express the inner spiritual urge."

There is a law not learned from books.

This is the law of divine enthusiasm. Dauntless and unconquerable, it brings into expression the wonderful quality we know as spiritual zeal. The action of spiritual zeal is one of the most powerful laws operative. To speak always fearlessly, truthfully, and courageously (with zeal) makes enthusiasm active and establishes an inner sense of confidence.

According to Fillmore:

"Spiritual zeal is one of the twelve fundamental powers of being and is symbolized by the apostle

Simon the Canaanite. In the body, its center is the medulla at the base of the brain. By centering the attention at this point, we realize the quickening power of the *Logos* (the Word). New zeal and courage find expression from the soul."

Since zeal is the power that ignites the other faculties to greater and greater activity, we must carefully search out hearts and minds in order to see whether our zeal springs from the spiritual consciousness or from the personal consciousness. If our incentive is from the spiritual consciousness, if we are working to serve, then zeal broadens our vision, makes us alert, and adds sweetness and strength to our whole being.

Otherwise, Fillmore tells us:

"If our zealous impulses derive from a personal consciousness (the ego) we are only driven to gain personal ends, to further our own interests, even at the expense of other people. Selfish zeal eventually burns up the life and substance of the mind and body, and leaves a starved, hungering soul. Emerson pictures a person intoxicated with personal zeal as 'inwardly drunk with a certain belief.'"

Let us stir up the gift of divine zeal within us, and we will find new inspiration, new ideas waiting to be born into the world.

How do you choose to stir up the power of zeal?

The power of zeal lends itself well to dynamic spiritual

and physical activity. Here is a soul quality that longs to be expressed in action in the outer world. When activating the quality of zeal in your life, do it with enthusiam and gusto. Here is the time to walk or run or dance your prayers and affirmations, using your body as an expression of zeal in action. Here is a time for you to speak aloud, chant, or sing your affirmative prayers. Zeal yearns to be expressed throughout the body temple.

Is there a special dream in your heart that you have not yet brought into fruition? Here is a perfect time to harness the energy of zeal to any undertaking—writing a book, building a house, pursuing an advanced degree, implementing a work project. The word "enthusiasm" has at its root—*en theos*—"of god." God is the divine spark of zeal working within you to activate enthusiastic energy, to inspire and motivate you toward the accomplishment of every dream. Zeal brings forth dreams into reality. Zeal married to divine order brings ideas into concrete reality. Zeal combined with the quality of divine wisdom is the teacher who molds impressionable minds with patience and love. Take the quality of zeal and couple it with any of the other soul qualities and they are multiplied in effectiveness. Zeal is the engine to true manifestation.

## ⚜ *Questions and Responses*

- What does the word "zeal" mean to you? How have you used zeal in your life recently? Is it time to activate the quality of zeal to complete a cherished dream? To work with passion and purpose? How has zeal shaped your interactions with others? Can you temper zeal with wisdom and order?

- Write three ways in which you can use zeal to be more effective in your life.
- Write three activities you want to accomplish and ask that zeal be your spiritual partner in manifesting these activities.
- Locate the zeal center within your body temple. Breathe zeal from its center within your body outward into your life. Let zeal be carried on the breath. Feel its power. Know its strength. Experience its energy. Thank zeal for being in your life. Ask that it manifest more and more for you in life-affirming, loving ways.
- Create your own acronym to remember the power of zeal. It could be: "Zest Expressed in Active Living" or "Zeal Enthusiastically Affirming Life."
- When you bring the word "zeal" into your life, remember and voice what it means to you. Affirm the power of zeal often. It will propel you forward into dynamic manifestation.

## ✤ Meditation

For the meditation in the silence, first take up the regenerative exercise given in the Introduction. Continue

The Spiritual Power of Zeal / 103

to allow the Presence to remain at the solar nerve center. Meditate:

"I am established in spiritual consciousness. I am zealous to serve God, to serve humanity."

Now let the Presence ascend to the base of the brain, the zeal center. Affirm:

"I am one with the ever-unfolding, ever-increasing Spirit of infinite courage, enthusiasm, and zeal."

Then let the Presence descend to the wisdom center, and meditate:

"Thou, O God, art always with me as indwelling infinite wisdom and spiritual judgment. I am zealous to know and to do Thy perfect will."

As the Presence ascends to the faith center, the pineal gland, at the center of the head, affirm:

"Through faith I see into the kingdom of the heavens. Through spiritual enthusiasm I work to bring that perfect kingdom into manifestation."

Let the Presence return to the zeal center, and affirm:

"The quickening, vitalizing, free-flowing enthusiasm of Spirit is mighty at work in me. I am transformed into newness of life."

As the Presence returns to the point at the back of the heart and stomach, affirm that you are zealous only to do the will of God. Close by quietly praying the Lord's Prayer. The conscious mind (front forehead) is aware of the entire regenerative exercise. Drop the attention down into the feet and beneath the feet, and realize perfect balance and poise.

*"Zeal is the mighty force that incites the winds, the tides, the storms; it urges the planet on its course, and spurs the ant to great exertion. To be without zeal is to be without the zest of living. Zeal and enthusiasm incite to glorious achievement in every aim and ideal that the mind conceives. Zeal is the impulse to go forward, the urge behind all things."*

## Chapter Eleven

# The Spiritual Power of Renunciation or Elimination
# Location: Abdominal Region
# Disciple: Thaddaeus

*"A change of mind effects a corresponding change in the body. If the thoughts are lifted up, the whole organism is raised to higher rates of vibration. If the system has been burdened with congestion of any kind, a higher life energy will set it into universal freedom. But there must be a renunciation or letting go of old thoughts before the new can find place in the consciousness. This is a psychological law, which has its outer expresssion in the intricate eliminative functions of the body."*

AFFIRMATION: "The Holy Spirit is now here, raising me to a consciousness of release. I realize that the cleansing, purifying power of the Holy Spirit is active in me."

There is a wonderful practical spiritual exercise that you may have been using for years. It consists of letting go of everything that you do not want, in order to make room for all that you do want. It is the law of creating a vacuum so that your new good can rush in to fill the space.

One of the things I used to do to practice this law was to periodically clean out my closets, my cabinets, my books. My children jokingly said, "For every book Mother gives away, ten rush in to take its place." I realized that this was a powerful affirmation that could be used in other areas of my life. I also realized that as I gave away the old, I didn't want ten more of the same thing. I didn't want the same thing at all. If I gave away the clutter in my life, I didn't need to be bombarded with new clutter. Instead, I found joy in creating a few beautiful things in my life, instead of a lot of stuff.

One of the ways to begin doing this is to give away something in your home every day for forty days. If a friend admires a pitcher, give it to her. If you see that the local homeless shelter has need of blankets, gather up all that you do not currently use. If a granddaughter is furnishing her first apartment, move the extra tables and desks out. If a women's shelter calls for donations, empty your closets.

There is a universal law that tells us, "You never lose anything by giving things away." I learned this lesson once and for all, when I began to sort, clear out, and pack for a move across the country. I was moving from a 2,000-square-foot house, plus attic and garage, to a (temporary) one-bedroom apartment that was expected to hold not only my office but my grandmother's antiques as well. I gave and I gave and I gave. After one attempt at a garage sale, early in the process, I realized that I was supposed to give and give again unstintingly, that this was indeed a spiritual exercise for me to learn. Up until the day that I left, I was still giving away, even after movers had come and gone. It was a powerful exercise for me.

A close friend asked me, "But what if you need these things where you are going? What if you miss what you have given away?"

"Then that will be a lesson too," I replied. So far I have missed only one item: an old orange desk chair that I used to sit in while I wrote my books. But I'm glad that I gave it away. It was needed elsewhere.

Of course, there is more to renunciation and elimination than material possessions. But when we give concretely, we can often see the results in the mundane world much faster. What else did I choose to give away? Old thought forms, depression, heaviness, frustration, fear, rage. I wanted to rid myself of areas in my emotional life that no longer served me (if they ever had).

According to Fillmore:

> "The action of the mind on the body is, in some of its aspects, similar to that of water on the earth. Living old thoughts over and over keeps the inlet of the new thoughts closed. Then begins crystallization . . ."

This task of giving up old thoughts instead of reliving them over and over is an ongoing process. It is a vital part of spiritual healing. If you take the same unhealed self into a new place, the new place will fill up with the same problems and the same results. You cannot have a new result if you continue operating in the same fashion.

The task is one of discernment. The more conscious and aware and clear you become, the easier it is to identify old thought forms and old emotional areas within your mind and heart that no longer serve you. Then choose again and once again what you will leave and give away, and what you will keep. I have kept my old friends and my dear loved ones. I have kept photograph albums that trace a lifetime, and precious memorabilia that speak to me of my heritage. But I don't need four closets, when one is plenty. I don't need 5,000 books (which I gave away in one day). The knowledge I need will come to my doorstep.

Sometimes, in the zeal of spiritual learning, we think that the more we know, the more we will have. And that more, more, more is always better. But Fillmore tells us that even in our zealous affirmations of truth principles, we can overload the mind with mental congestion, which manifests as congested conditions in the body. Who has not been overloaded with mental and emotional stress, which manifests in the body as a cold? The eliminative functions of the body cannot work when the system is overloaded with too much. Even when I write my books, and want to continue for two or three more hours, there comes a time when my head says, "No," because I have overloaded my circuits. I need to pause and do something physical.

According to Fillmore:

"Thus it is possible to overload the mind, as one overloads the stomach. Thoughts must be digested in a manner similar to the way in which food is digested. An eagerness to gain knowledge without proper digestion and assimilation ends in mental congestion."

Renunciation and elimination need not be a painful process. Each time we take in a new breath, we accept the new life that is coming into our bodies. Each time we exhale, we are eliminating the old. So renunciation and elimination are a simple process, as easy as breathing in and breathing out. By prayerfully concentrating on the quality of renunciation, you will easily let go of the old and lay hold of the new.

According to Fillmore:

"In the lower part of the back, near the base of the spinal column, is a ganglionic nerve center. It is symbolized by Jesus' apostle (Thaddaeus), and it presides over the elimination of waste from the body temple. It eliminates error thoughts from the mind and expands the good. If it is spiritually quickened, it has the power to perform a wonderful work which establishes a freedom in soul and body consciousness, giving tone and strength and elasticity to the whole man [woman]. Letting go of the old, in an orderly and decisive manner, at the same time laying hold of the new, engenders a sweetness and lightness in the whole being."

Letting go of the old is also an important step in the forgiveness process. We are continually creating more of our spiritual self and casting out of our mind and body all that is no longer right for us.

According to Fillmore:

"Spirit is constantly infusing us with more of itself. . . . The forgiving love of God is an important factor in the eliminative process. When we know that we are forgiven for any errors or mistakes that we have made, we are opening the way for the fulfillment of the law. Personality is discarded and spiritual forces begin to renew and rejuvenate. Letting go of the old, inrushing of the new—when the law of forgiveness is satisfied, our whole being draws new life and strength and power from the one divine source; it throws off the old."

This is a constant daily process: that of choosing consciously what we will keep and what we will discard. If we choose to be healthy, happy, prosperous, we must learn to do healthy, hearty, and positive thinking. We must not be dominated by another's will, or let another do our thinking for us. If we try to hold on and let go at the same time, renunciation and elimination in both mind and body are weakened, negative, irregular. We must learn to recognize and then let go of a grasping personality and old possessive ideas in order for there to be harmony in body, mind, emotions, and spirit.

The remedy is to relax, to let go. The words of Truth that you have affirmed must have time to work out in the subconsciousness.

You are making your body temple a dwelling place for the soul. The passing away of the old and the incoming of the new are results of the outworking of spiritual law. Every experience aids in establishing more firmly your identity in Spirit; with greater freedom and power you are brought nearer to your goal of perfection—health in mind and body.

## ✼ *Questions and Responses*

- What three physical things can I let go of in my life today?
- Do I need to replace these things, or simply let them go?
- What three mental ideas have served their purpose, and need to be discarded from my mind?
- What three old emotional thought forms are no longer helpful to me?
- What habits do I need to break? When am I willing to begin to break these habits?
- What new ideas and emotional understanding can I put in the place of the old?

- How can I create a vacuum in my life for new good to rush in? Am I willing, at this time, to give away forty things for forty days? If so, I will begin. If not, why not? When am I likely to be willing to do this exercise?

The spiritual quality of renunciation and elimination is extremely powerful. It is an agent for change in every area of your life. Activate it for good, and you will be amazed and grateful to God for the results.

## ✢ Meditation

For a regenerative meditation in the silence, first follow the one given in the Introduction. Continue to allow the Presence to dwell at the great solar nerve center, realizing that the indwelling Christ in action is standing in your midst, controlling, directing power, saying, "Come unto me—I will give you rest." As these words penetrate your consciousness, you will be letting go of all weariness, all doubt, all fear; you will feel a lightness and freedom throughout your whole being. Hold this thought:

"I gladly let go of the old. I am expanded with the new life of Spirit."

Allow the Presence to ascend to the heart, the love center. Affirm:

## The Spiritual Power of Renunciation / 113

"The forgiving love of Spirit cleanses, purifies, and strengthens me."

Dwell on this thought, relax more and more, concentrating on the regions of the heart and solar plexus. Be sure the conscious mind is fully aware of the work being done.

Now allow the Presence to return to the center of renunciation, located at the lower end of the spinal column. Meditate upon this:

"The forgiving love of Spirit cleanses, purifies, and strengthens me."

Let the Presence ascend to the small of the back, the center of strength. Affirm:

"I gladly let go of weak, worn-out thoughts in mind and body. The joy of the Lord is my strength."

Imagine the Presence radiating back of the navel, the order center, and meditate:

"Every function and every organ of my body is now working in perfect harmony with spiritual law. Divine order is established in my mind and body."

Let the Presence descend again to the center of elimination and praise God, giving thanks that His spiritual word is active throughout your whole being. You are joyously working with the cleansing, discriminating, purifying power of inner being.

To conclude, allow the Presence to ascend to the great solar nerve center and repeat the Lord's Prayer.

Always be conscious of the light of Spirit descending continually from the spiritual center at the crown of the head. You should in truth be conscious of every step taken in the entire exercise.

After the close of the exercise, throw the attention down into the feet and beneath, and into the palms of the hands. Realize perfect poise and balance throughout your whole being.

> *"The faculty of renunciation is twofold in nature: It eliminates error and it expands the good. The expansion of the holy and sacred divine spark is an integral part of our spiritual development.*
>
> *"Our bodies are divine, therefore every activity of the body is fundamentally divine. We must know this, realize it daily, if we would make our body a fit dwelling place for the Holy Spirit."*

## Chapter Twelve

# The Spiritual Power of Generative Life
# Location: Generative Function
# Disciple: Judas

*"In the phenomenal world, life is the energy that propels all forms to action. Life in the body is like electricity in a motor.... Life is not in itself intelligent—it requires the directive power of an entity that knows where and how to apply its force, in order to get the best results. The engineer of the life force in the body ... is the life ego; this is the consciousness of life in the organism."*

AFFIRMATION: "The Holy Spirit is now here raising me to a consciousness of everlasting life. I am filled with vitalizing, powerful energy."

The metaphysical disciple that corresponds to the Life center within us is called Judas. Why? I asked, and asked again, when I first came across Fillmore's interpretation. Why would something as vital, powerful, and sweet as the life energy within us carry the name of the disciple who stands for betrayal? After meditating on this for some time, I came to the conclusion that it is precisely the nature of betrayal that we must recognize and root out of our consciousness in order to allow the center of life within us to resurrect into a more viable, spiritualized form.

While Judas is the metaphysical disciple mentioned by Fillmore to correspond to this faculty, Fillmore seldom refers to Judas again. He only refers to the generative life of the organism as it moves from sense sensations to spiritual awareness and regeneration. You can compare this to the way in which we betray ourselves again and again and experience betrayal in the outer world (like Judas betraying Christ), until we learn to call on the Christ Consciousness within as the rejuvenator of our lives, the generative power, the wellspring, the spiritual redeemer, rather than on all the outer material events that may have betrayed and victimized us in the past. This center of life within the body temple also corresponds to the *Kundalini,* the serpent power in ancient esoteric texts, that, once awakened through prayer and meditation, must be mastered as part of our ongoing spiritual discipline or it will overwhelm us.

According to Fillmore:

> "Potentially, life's problems are already worked out for us, but we do not always consciously know this. We do not strive for soul unfoldment without the desire for greater understanding and a greater de-

gree of life activity. Yet when we develop the ability to lay hold of understanding, through the inner push to greater achievement, we find that Spirit has gone before us and accomplished the real work for us. Life's problems consist chiefly in awakening the consciousness of spiritual powers of being, acquiring a mental grasp of them, and transmuting chaos and confusion into light and joy."

How do we begin to transmute inner chaos and confusion into a life of light and joy? In addition to the regenerative exercises delineated in this chapter, there are a number of questions we can begin to ask ourselves and, in meditation, allow the answers to come to us. These are not questions about the betrayals of others, but about self-betrayal. We can also hunt for a new image of renewing life to replace old patterns of self-pity, self-hatred, and self-betrayal. Then we are replacing the Judas within with images of eternal life.

Beyond betrayal is regeneration and resurrection. When I close my eyes and allow a new image of regneration to come to me, the idea of a tree of life springs into full consciousness. Fillmore himself wrote of this wonderful tree of life when describing several centers of the body temple and how they interact together. It is a wonderful image of regeneration and renewal for all of us.

According to Fillmore:

"The wonderful tree of life brings forth much fruit, symbolizing the unlimited power of Spirit to increase. The tree of life symbolically represents the soul's energy and life in the nervous system.

"There are two great branches to this tree of life: the sympathetic nervous system and the cerebrospinal nervous system. The great ganglia of the sympathetic system regulate the functions of respiration, circulation, and digestion. The nerve centers near the heart and stomach are the central nervous stations for this system. These nerve centers enable us to feel joy or sadness, health or sickness. The cerebrospinal system consists of the brain and the spinal cord, with branches to all parts of the body. This system empowers the body with the ability to move, to act, to express life force."

Your whole body is a tree of life, continually renewing itself from its roots to the crown. It regenerates through each of the twelve powers and continues its work through all the spiritual seasons of your life. This redeeming process is continually carried on throughout the whole being.

By envisioning yourself as a beautiful and ever-renewing tree of life, you create a spiritual idea that contradicts all old thoughts of betrayal and victimization. You then teach your mind to see this new idea. You become the new spiritual idea. When you do this, Fillmore tells us:

"The spiritual idea works in the human notions that have already been formed, and mental standards are revolutionized. The intellect transforms, sharpens, shines; it becomes a fit tool of Spirit."

So do you, too, become a fit tool of Spirit through the regenerative exercises that follow. Instead of betrayal of your highest ideals and purposes, you are transformed into new life, new energy, new power and possibilities. With God's help, you become your own agent of resurrection.

## ✲ Questions and Responses

- How have I betrayed the life force within my body?
- How have I betrayed my talents, my abilities?
- How have I betrayed the life that God has given me? By reflecting on these questions, which I ask you to do now, we begin to see that most betrayals are not visited on other people, nor are we betrayed by others. Instead, most betrayals are self-betrayals, perpetrated, however unconsciously, upon ourselves and our potentialities.
- What is your deepest dream?
- What is your soul's purpose?
- How can you best serve? These are also questions to ask yourself, even as you speak words of regeneration and renewal.

## ✣ Meditation

The meditation for regenerative life is of great importance. It is longer and more intricate than our preceding exercises. Begin with the exercise given in the Introduction, realizing that you are perfectly relaxed in mind and body. Allow the Presence to dwell at the back of the heart and stomach, the great solar nerve center, and affirm:

"My life is one with God, and all my substance is quickened and increased."

Feel the new life that is quickening within you, flowing out through the breast and down into the innermost part of your body. The outpouring of spiritual life is gently descending from the spiritual center at the crown of the head. Let the Presence drop to the lower abdomen, the generative center. As you approach this center, think of the pure, strong, sweet life of Spirit. Know that right now this regenerated life is waiting to do its perfect work in you. Every coarse impulse of soul and body is transmuted into divine purity of life and purpose. Imagine the Presence being diffused throughout the life organs. Affirm:

"I am Spirit. I am the resurrection and the life."

Be aware of a great purifying, transmuting power beginning to work in you. Allow the Presence to return to the solar nerve center, and reaffirm: "I am Spirit. I am the resurrection and the life."

Next allow the Presence to ascend to the power center at the root of the tongue. Affirm:

"All power is given to me in mind and body."

Allow the Presence to ascend into the front forehead, to the center of will and understanding. Affirm:

"I have perfect understanding of life. I am divinely guided in all my ways."

Let the Presence descend to the order center at the back of the navel. Affirm:

"The law of the Spirit of life creates divine order within me."

Allow the Presence to drop to the life center at the base of the spine. Reaffirm:

"I am Spirit. I am the resurrection and the life."

There is a great regenerative work going on within you, and you will know it. Impulses of sense consciousness are being transmuted into spiritual understanding. The essence of the very food you have taken into the body is being refined and transmuted into a higher radiation of upbuilding energy. The process of cooperation with the Holy Spirit has begun, lifting up and distributing new life and force to all parts of the soul and body. The life in the body ascends the spinal cord and flows out over thousands of nerve tributaries leading from the spinal cord to every part of the body. This is the tree of life within you.

Continue the exercise, sensing the Presence of new, refined life at the base of the spinal cord. Let this all-knowing Power lift at a point halfway between the base of the spinal cord and the small of the back. Allow the Presence to dwell there for several moments and discover a great harmonizing, equalizing sensation. Affirm:

> "The peace and harmony of the Holy Spirit in me is doing its perfect work. I confidently and joyfully rest."

Allow the Presence to lift up the life essence to the small of the back, the strength center. Be aware that new life energy is being dispensed to the innermost parts of the body and to the outermost rim of consciousness. Realize that there is an ever-increasing flow as you affirm:

> "I am made strong and pure through the nourishing life of Spirit at work within me."

Let the Presence carry the life force upward until it reaches the great solar nerve center, where it will mightily flood the consciousness with life energy, pouring over into all the vital parts of the body.

There will be a new activity in the wisdom center and the love center as the head and the heart learn to work harmoniously. Realize that a generous supply of this renewed life energy is merged with wisdom and love, and is being freely dispersed through invisible channels to the front forehead. A keen, unclouded mind is dominating your conscious thinking. The Presence will continue to lift up a generous portion of the life essence to the base of the brain, the center of zeal, where it will do a mighty work. Affirm:

"I enthusiastically express the wisdom and peace of infinite life."

Allow the Presence to carry this new life energy over a set of motor nerves leading from the zeal center to the eyes and into the crown of the head. Realize:

"The light and intellignce of Spirit are now manifest in me. I see clearly."

Allow the Presence to carry this new life energy to the nerves in the ears. Affirm:

"My ears are open. I hear the voice of Spirit."

Following the same process, let the new energy flow to the nose. Affirm:

"The discrimination and purity of Spirit are active in me."

Allow the Presence to carry the life current to the mouth, the root of the tongue. Affirm:

"I am free with the freedom of Spirit."

You will remember that the throne of power is situated at the root of the tongue, extending down into the neck. When the Presence carries new life from the zeal center to the throne of power, it sets up a mighty vibration that affects the whole sympathetic nervous system. New life and energy are imparted to the digestive tract, and the voice and teeth are strengthened.

When the Presence carries the new life current from the zeal center at the base of the brain to the throne of power at the root of the tongue, the union of the life current with the power energy manufactures a new element.

Allow the Presence to make this union between the zeal and power centers. Affirm:

"I am a new woman [man] in Spirit."

Quietly allow the Presence to descend to the great solar nerve center. Close the exercise by repeating the Lord's Prayer.

Be perfectly relaxed in mind and body, aware of the entire meditation exercise. Throw the attention into the

# The Spiritual Power of Generative Life / 125

feet and beneath, and also into the palms of the hands. This tends to keep you in perfect poise and balance.

Go forth in your new life consciousness, expressing it in every function of your whole being.

*"Back of all is God's eternal plan; our place in the world is waiting for us, and Spirit is with us every step of the way. As we continue toward victory, a truer understanding of life appears. We dissolve inertia and we are filled with new confidence, new life activity to spur us onward. We develop spiritual powers by working out of lethargic states of consciousness. We cease to struggle, cease resisting and we learn to serve the forces of life with new strength and trust. The adversary who has held us all in bondage for so long—our own belief in appearances (our Judas)—is at the mercy of spiritual light and understanding."*

## Conclusion

# The Twelve Spiritual Powers United

*"A change in ideas must necessarily produce a change in the body, and there is a perfect response in every center of consciousness when Spirit has been welcomed as the rightful inhabitant of the body."*

AFFIRMATION: "I am one with my twelve spiritual powers united by God."

Here is the full meditation on the twelve powers, representing all the spiritual centers in the body. This full meditation is expressed daily in your spiritual practice, after the previous weeks of activating each individual divine inner power and expressing it in your life.

> The I AM throne, known as the God Consciousness or Christ Consciousness, is the spiritual center of the body located at the crown of the head. It is through the I AM that pure intelligence and light descend from on high into the conscious mind in the front forehead. The head is literally lit from within. Imagine this flow descending to the faith

## The Twelve Spiritual Powers United / 127

center in the pineal gland at the center of the head. Divine inspiration and ideas pour forth from divine mind through the I AM of the individual into consciousness, where they are met with faith and freed to activate substance and manifest good.

This flow of life descends into the cardiac center (which radiates love) and the great solar nerve center behind the heart and stomach. Here the divine power begins to activate, for this is the center of divine manifestation. Here the network of energy channels reach out to all twelve spiritual centers. The throne of the divine is the I AM center, where inspiration is born, while the home of the manifest divine, the disseminator of these divine ideas into substance, is at the great solar nerve center.

In this meditation, we are seeking to unfold into our lives the fundamental faculties of Divine Mind: faith, strength, wisdom, love, power, imagination, understanding, will, order, zeal, renunciation, and life.

This manifestation of the divine begins to shape the perfect body temple as well as our perfect outer environment. It works to develop itself and the other spiritual powers through the inspiration of the I AM direction.

For the meditation in the silence, concentrate your attention in the crown of the head. Through the I AM, realize that you are releasing infinite knowledge into your consciousness. These radiations penetrate your soul and body. You consciously sense the emanation of Spirit as pure light, pure intelligence, descending through you from the I AM center. Feel the Spirit working within every cell and fiber of your body temple. The emanation of Spirit flows to the faith center and the conscious mind is illumined.

You are suffused with the soft flow of infinite intelligence. Its light moves through you, descending to contact another current from below, the earthly current. The all-knowing power of Spirit transforms thoughts from the earthly current. There is no fear, lack, anger, guilt, shame, or sickness here. There is only courage, abundance, peace, justice, wisdom, health, and love.

By understanding the earthly current, you can begin to transform it in your mind as you continue to work with spiritual Truth. Gradually, as it ascends, permeating and penetrating your whole being, it meets with the downpouring of light from on high. It is transformed in you, and your life will reflect this transformation. The renewed earthly current goes to the great solar center of you, called the manifest God Consciousness or Christ Consciousness. This is where your true core self resides. Activating this spiritual consciousness creates new power and ability in you.

Now imagine the ascending current rising from beneath the feet, flowing to the seat of this core self, this spiritual consciousness within you. Dwell here. Meditate on the fundamental ideas in God-Mind. Realize that rays of light from God-Mind through the I AM center, to the great solar nerve center, are now radiating to all points of spiritual power within the body. Develop each of these faculties with these blessings:

Declare to the faith center in the pineal gland: "I have faith in God." Return to the core center of your being with this message.

Declare to the strength center at the small of the back: "God is the strength of my life." Return to the core center of your being with this message.

Declare to the power center at the root of the tongue: "I am peaceful and poised in divine power." Return to the core center of your being with this message.

Declare to the imagination center, between the eyes: "I am created in the image and after the likeness of God." Return to the core center of your being with this message.

Declare to the understanding center in the front forehead: "My understanding is of God." Return to the core center of your being with this message.

Declare to the center of will, also in the front forehead: "My will is to obey God's will." Return to the core center of your being with this message.

Declare to the order center, behind the navel: "I am one with divine order." Return to the core center of your being with this message.

Declare to the center of zeal at the base of the brain: "I am zealous in my efforts to be in perfect accord with infinite wisdom." Return to the core center of your being with this message.

Declare to the renunciation center at the base of the spinal column: "I gladly let go of the old. I gladly lay hold of the new." Return to the core center of your being with this message.

Declare to the life center in the lower abdomen: "My life is one with Christ in God." Return to the core center of your being with this message.

Through the center of love, God radiates good. Declare to your whole being: "I am actively living in God's love." Return to the core center of your being with this message.

Spiritual life radiates from within you outward. Its blessings light the spiritual centers in your body. You are now consciously aware of the experience of light. Dwell at the center of your being and repeat the Lord's Prayer.

The light of Spirit descends as new inspiration. It deals perfectly and powerfully with the ascending earthly current; it transforms earthly thoughts to Truth. You now experience perfect relaxation in body and mind. You are a spiritual being, now clothed in a body of light. You have firmly established your I AM power and dominion, and all twelve faculties express themselves through the God consciousness in you. You are radiant with new life and inspiration. Your feet are planted firmly on the rock of spiritual understanding. You are a new person, open to good, open to give. You know that you must use the ideas and inspirations you receive, for the life of God is to express all good. You will radiate the light from within your spiritual core self into your world and affairs. You will open the way to more good. You will express the Spirit of God in all that you think, say, and do. You are one with your good. You are one with the Spirit of God.

*"If the energy of Spirit were instantly poured into the body, it would destroy the organism because of the impurities of the flesh, but by and through the evolutionary adjustment of the natural [woman] man, the Spirit not only preserves but raises up the substance and life of the organism. The purpose of our spiritual thoughts ... down in the body ... is to raise up the body—gradually to infuse into it a more enduring life and substance. At the same time our spiritual thoughts get the substance ... that is to sustain their existence in the world of phenomena."*

## ✣ Summing Up

*"The process of forming a soul may be compared to the development, in a photographic negative, of the image that has been imprinted upon the sensitive plate but cannot be seen until it has been put through a regular developing process."*

The body is composed of building blocks of light, with twelve main centers of soul power. The body itself is stepped-down light, light made material, light made matter, in the manifest world.

Our task as spiritual beings encased in human bodies is to awaken these twelve soul qualities and use them for our work in the world.

We do this in many ways, depending on our level of

awareness. We do this by identifying, affirming, and contemplating each soul quality. We do this with right motivation, service, and an increasing call to our true character. We do this with deep reflection and affirmative prayer. We do this with a disciplined spiritual practice that, in and of itself, builds the quality and quantity of light available to us. We do this gently and tenderly and prayerfully, with great mercy and loving kindness to ourselves. We strip away the old; we let go of density. With each breath of light, with each thought of light, we refine our body temples. We clear and forgive our emotional body. We make our minds into lighted lamps. It is a continuous process, this one of accessing, identifying, and calling upon these metaphysical disciples. It leads to great and powerful change. It is a lifelong process. It is the act of transformation itself.

There are many roads to the soul. This is one. It is simple, sweet, prayerful. It does not ask you to embrace dogma, to judge your fellow man or woman, to sacrifice your reason. It asks only that you look within you for the spark of God. It asks that you identify with the highest and the best that you can conceive. It asks that you believe in God, by whatever name and in whatever way your soul requires. It asks that you bring spiritual understanding into all that you do in the outer world.

Can you be transformed by the renewing of your mind, your emotions, your body temple? Yes, yes, and again yes. Your soul awaits to awaken to its divine design. Your soul awaits.

*"There can be but one course for the obedient devotee. If you have surrendered all to omnipresent wisdom, you must take as final what it tells you. You will find that its guidance is the right course for you and, in the end, that it was the only course that you could possibly have taken...."*

# SUGGESTIONS FOR FURTHER STUDY

Unity School of Christianity is located at 1901 NW Blue Parkway, Unity Village, MO 64065-0001. It was founded in 1889 and offers retreats, ministerial training, publications, and Silent Unity (an ongoing prayer circle that continues twenty-four hours a day).

Tel: (816) 534-3550

Unity publishes *Daily Word, Daily Word in Braille,* and *La Palabra Diario* (*Daily Word* in Spanish). *Daily Word* is translated into nine different languages and reaches millions of people all over the world. Unity also publishes *Unity Magazine* and a number of books and study guides through Unity Books. You can find a local Unity church or study center in thousands of cities around the world. Call Unity at the number above for the one closest to your area. For magazine subscriptions or book orders, call customer service at (816) 969-2069 or toll free (800) 669-0282.

Other classic works by Charles Fillmore include:

*The Revealing Word*   *Jesus Christ Heals*
*Dynamics for Living*   *Atom-Smashing Power of Mind*
*Prosperity*   *Christian Healing*